Help, Lord! I'm Having a Senior Moment

Help, Lord!
I'm Having a Senior Moment

Notes to God on Growing Older

KAREN O'CONNOR

Regal

From Gospel Light
Ventura, California, U.S.A.

PUBLISHED BY REGAL BOOKS
FROM GOSPEL LIGHT
VENTURA, CALIFORNIA, U.S.A.
Regal PRINTED IN THE U.S.A.

Regal Books is a ministry of Gospel Light, a Christian publisher dedicated to serving the local church. We believe God's vision for Gospel Light is to provide church leaders with biblical, user-friendly materials that will help them evangelize, disciple and minister to children, youth and families.

It is our prayer that this Regal book will help you discover biblical truth for your own life and help you meet the needs of others. May God richly bless you.

Originally published by Servant Publications in 2002.

Cover design: Paul Higdon, Minneapolis, Minnesota

Library of Congress Cataloging-in-Publication Data

O'Connor, Karen, 1938–
  Help, Lord! I'm having a senior moment : notes to God about growing
older / Karen O'Connor.
    p. cm.
Originally published: 2002.
  ISBN 0-8307-3440-6
  1. Christian aged–Religious life. 2. Aging–Religious
aspects–Christianity. I. Title.
  BV4580.O36 2003
  242'.65–dc22   2003026484

6 7 8 9 10 11 12 13 14 15 16 17 18 / 12 11 10 09 08 07 06 05 04

Rights for publishing this book in other languages are contracted by Gospel Light World-wide, the international nonprofit ministry of Gospel Light. Gospel Light Worldwide also provides publishing and technical assistance to international publishers dedicated to producing Sunday School and Vacation Bible School curricula and books in the languages of the world. For additional information, visit www.gospellightworldwide.org; write to Gospel Light Worldwide, P.O. Box 3875, Ventura, CA 93006; or send an e-mail to info@gospellightworldwide.org.

For my husband,
Charles Flowers, my favorite senior.

Contents

Contents

Moments We'd Rather Forget / 81

Contents

Contents

Acknowledgments

The author wishes to thank the following men and women for contributing their ideas and experiences—all of which have been woven into the fabric of this book.

Donna Adee • Alice Adler • Beverly J. Anderson • Barbara Anson • Millie Barger • Virginia Baty • Twila Belk • Crane Delbert Bennett • Mike S. Bolley • Sybil W. Brennecke • Barbara Bryden • Charlotte Burkholder • Jessie Butler • LeAnn Campbell • Penelope Carlevato • Kitty Chappell • Pamela Christian • Joan Collett • Laurie Copeland • Rebecca Clark Culpepper • Marlene Depler • Karla Downing • Lindsey Downing • Susie Duncan • Patricia Evans • Eva Marie Everson • Olga Flores • Charles Flowers • Connie Fowler • Freda Fullerton • Nancy Gibbs • Verda Glick • Beverly Hamel • Judith Harris • Esther Herriott • Cecile Higgins • Bernice Jenkins • Margaret Johnson • Paulette Johnson • Janis Keehn • Teresa Bell Kindred • Sandi Knode • Paul Krieger • Carole Lewis • Nancy Merical • Sherrie Murphree • Jeannie Myers • June O'Connor • Yvonne Ortega • Richard Perkins • Cindy Plewinski • Eunice Ratzlaff • Kimberly Ripley • Karen Robertson • Martha Rogers • Betty Rosian • Jeanne Roth • Dayle Shockley • Annette Smith • Betty Southard • Maureen Stirsman • Karen Taylor • June Varnum • Claudia Ward • Mildred Wenger • Lonnie West • Kathleen Dale Wright • Connie Bertelsen Young • Jeanne Zornes

Senior Moments
by Karen Taylor

This book tells not of youngsters
and the way they spend their days.
It's all about us old folks
and our fuddy-duddy ways.

Sometimes it's hard to figure
what life is all about.
My brain is finally working,
now my body's giving out.

Or perhaps I'm right on schedule
for a very special date.
My body's running right on time,
but my mind is running late.

Well, what does it all matter
in the scheme and theme of things
as long as I find comfort
in the joy that laughter brings?

I'll share these tales with others,
so they might find laughter too.
You can bet your bottom dollar
the tales will all be true.

And when you've finished reading
about folks like you and me,
you'll be surprised and pleased to know
you're as normal as can be!

My mother-in-law Ada often said, "Growing old is not for sissies!" My husband and I smiled whenever she said it. Then quickly we reassured her that she was young at heart and that's all that mattered. Easy for us to say. At the time neither of us had crossed the bridge from older-middle age to older-older age. We thought we were doing her a favor by cheering her up—hoping to keep her eyes and her mind off the physical limitations that had set in.

That was twenty-some years ago. Today, we have a much better understanding of what Ada was talking about. It takes grit and courage and prayer to face the other side of fifty and sixty and seventy. Some days I find myself calling out to God, "Help, Lord. I'm having a senior moment!" I smile when I say it— because I like to look at life through a positive lens—but the reality is there. I have plenty of zest for living, but still there are changes—those "senior moments"—when the name of someone I know well, or the precise word I'm looking for, doesn't come to mind as quickly as it used to. I need more sleep these days and I give myself more time to drive or walk or read or eat. I'm not in as much of a hurry as I once was—because I can't be!

I hope the notes to God in the following pages (some of my own, and some based on the funny and touching contributions I've received from other seniors—men and women) will encourage you, cause you to smile, laugh, maybe even sigh and shed a tear, as you recognize familiar situations, emotions, frustrations and joys that are as true for you as they are for me—and countless others.

Whether you're under the pile or standing on top, it's my hope and prayer that this book will offer you comfort, sympathy, companionship and plenty of good humor! Allow the Lord to encourage and strengthen you, and to confirm in your heart his deep love for you in all your comings and goings. There is only one who can meet our deepest needs— Jesus Christ himself. Through all of our moments as seniors, we can count on him to make good his promise never to leave us nor forsake us (Heb 13:5).

Funny Moments

The cheerful heart has a continual feast.

PROVERBS 15:15

Money Laundering

Dear God:

For twenty years the laundry room has been off-limits to me. I've been instructed—and you're my witness—that my knowledge of how to wash, dry, fold and iron clothes is so lacking as to disqualify me from even *auditing* Household Management 101.

Furthermore, my husband has made it clear that he could not only teach the course but run the entire university department on such matters! You've seen him in action, Lord. This guy is worth his weight in soapsuds! There's nothing he likes better than the rhythmic pounding of a washing machine whirling socks and shirts into submission. Even the sheets snap to attention when he comes round the bend and through the bedroom door.

In our house, it's *Charles* in *Charge*—of all things pima and percale, rayon and nylon, velvet and velour! Even his dresser and closet spaces are fit for inspection any time of the day or night. A two-finger space separates each shirt on pristine white hangers. Socks are lined up in the drawer from gray to blue to brown to black, and nary an argyle shall dare come between them.

The hamper is never more than half full. And the crease in his pants matches the crease in his brow!

So imagine my shock and his chagrin, when I walked into the laundry room today. There he stood holding a soggy lump of leather in one hand and a mass of wet bills and dripping credit cards in the other. Yep! The man is up to no good—I caught him laundering our money!

BUT I WANT to keep him anyway, Lord! Thank you for giving me a husband I can count on and laugh with.

Right—and Proud of It

Dear God:

Is it time to hire a bookkeeper? A secretary? An aide? After what happened this week I think so—though it did work in my favor. (Smile!) You know I'm careful about not mixing my personal funds with the church's funds. When I do spend my own money for supplies or services, it's only right that I get reimbursed, as the other directors and I agreed.

But I wonder what they'd think of my latest stunt. As I was updating my personal check register this morning, I discovered that several weeks ago I'd written a check from my own checking account to reimburse myself!

This is one of those "moments" I'd rather forget. Fortunately, I usually do. Saves a lot of embarrassment. Until it happens again ...

"Where are my credit cards?" my wife asked yesterday, as we were almost ready to walk out the door for church. I was planning to drop her off at the mall after the service so she could pick up a birthday gift for our granddaughter.

Arlette was clearly irritated with her forgetfulness. As she stood at the breakfast counter and rummaged through her purse for the second time, I spotted her cards. Aha! I cleared my throat to get her attention, and then chuckled out loud.

"What's so funny?" she barked.

"There they are, on top of the counter, right under your nose," I crowed.

She picked up the cards in silence and off we went.

I settled into the driver's seat and backed down the drive. It seemed a good time to remind Arlette of a few things.

"Before you leave the house," I instructed, "you should make sure you put everything you need in its proper place. Preferably do this the night before so you won't waste time the following morning. Then before you start the car," I added, "you should make sure you're comfortable. Check your seat to be sure it's positioned appropriately. Check the steering wheel. Check to see that your seat belt is fastened properly. Check all the instruments."

At this point my wife was breathing deeply. She seemed annoyed at my Sunday sermon but she said nothing. Then halfway to church she exclaimed, "Oh, no! I can't believe this. I forgot my Bible."

"As I was saying," I continued. "If you had put your Bible in the car last night ... well, it's too late to go back for it now," I reprimanded. "You can share mine. You see *I* always put *my* Bible in the car on Saturday night. That way I don't forget it."

I glanced at Arlette. She was drumming her fingers against her purse. "You should ...," I stopped mid-sentence. I could tell I was in hot water.

But still—I *knew* I was right. As I swung into the church parking lot I took a deep breath. There's nothing to worry about, I consoled myself silently. If a person just *thinks ahead*, he or she won't forget the essentials—like credit cards and one's Bible, for heaven's sake.

We got out of the car, and as was my habit, I checked my back pocket to be sure my wallet was in place.

Suddenly my face turned hot and my palms were wet.

"Oh, no," I muttered. "I forgot my wallet. My credit cards and my driver's license are at home."

"Is that so?" my wife queried with great calm.

It was all she really needed to say.

WHAT I NEEDED to say, Lord, was, "Please forgive me," but I hung on to my pride. I regret that now. I know it's never too late to apologize. Excuse me, Lord, while I take care of some important business with my wife.

Check at the Front Desk

Dear God:

Sometimes I get full of myself and I'm cocky about the life I've lived and all of my accomplishments—engineer, senior manager, civic leader, husband and father, award-winning researcher. I can hardly believe I'm seventy-two already—but I'm glad I made it this far. Thank you for giving me so much time. And when I get "too big for my britches," as my mother used to say, pull me down to where I ought to be.

Reminds me of the story I heard the other day about an elderly man who was once a famous, award-winning athlete in track and field. He had a room full of plaques and statues and framed certificates. Years after retiring from competition, he was invited to deliver the keynote address for an awards banquet for young athletes. After finishing his presentation, the audience jumped to their feet and chanted his name over and over! He walked out feeling like a kid again, heady with memories of the bygone days when he was king of the one hundred-yard dash.

As he shook hands with admirers at the end of the evening, he told them of his plan to spend his last years visiting the elderly at various health care and retirement facilities. Because of his age, he knew the children in hospital wards wouldn't know him as a celebrity, but he was sure people in his age bracket would! He was convinced he could encourage them with his stories of success and even show off some of his trophies. He could hardly wait for his first visit.

The following week he arrived at a nursing home and noticed immediately the halls were empty except for one elderly lady in a wheelchair. He got her attention with a cheery, "Good morning!" Then he asked, "Ma'am, do you know who I am?"

She looked at him with pale blue eyes and smiled. "No, but if you go to the front desk someone there will tell you," she replied in a quivering voice.

OH LORD, spare me from being my own public relations agent. Help me remember that my identity is in you—and you alone. Who am I? A child of the most high God—and that's more than I deserve and nothing I can take credit for.

More Than One Way ...

Dear God:

I like this one! An older man from Phoenix phoned his son in New York with some bad news. "Son, I don't mean to ruin your day, but I need to tell you something important. Your mother and I are divorcing. Forty-five years of misery is enough for both of us."

"Dad, do you realize what you're saying? You can't be serious," the son pleaded.

"It's true. We can't take another minute of being together. I don't want to discuss it any further. It's settled. Call your sister in Chicago and let her know." The older man hung up.

Frantic, the son called his sister, who exploded on the phone. "Like heck they're getting divorced," she shouted. "Sit tight. I'll handle this."

She called her father in Phoenix and yelled into the phone. "You are *not* getting divorced. Don't do a single thing until I get there. I'm calling Dick back, and we'll both be there tomorrow. Until then, stay put," she shouted. *"Do you hear me?"* Then she hung up.

The older man put down the phone and turned to his wife, a wry smile crossing his face as he spoke. "Okay," he said, "they're coming for Thanksgiving and paying their own fares. Now what do we tell them for Christmas?"

LORD, YOU REMIND us in your Word: "Listen to your father, who gave you life, and do not despise your mother when she is old" (Prv 23:22). Surely your wisdom and the parents' good humor will knit their hearts together!

Butter Up

Dear God:

I need to talk to you about something. I think I'm losing it—really.

It all started when Dr. Simpson called my husband into his office after his physical exam.

"John, your cholesterol count is close to 300," the doctor said. "I recommend you cut down on the eggs and hold the butter. Avoid the saturated fats, too. We'll check again in three months."

Easy for the doctor to say, right, Lord? He doesn't live at our house. We love butter. No hydrogenated margarine for us. We like the real thing. Butter on toast, on warm rolls, on sweet buns after church on Sunday.

Of course, I don't have to give it up. My cholesterol count is just fine: 170. So there, Doctor So-and-so! I thought.

But then a pang of guilt overtook me. I should support my husband, I mused. If he can't have butter for a while, then perhaps I need to give it up, too. Then I decided the best thing to do was keep it out of sight—put it somewhere he'd never think to look. I made up my mind. I'd find the perfect hiding place for my stick of butter.

But now I think *I'm* the one who needs a doctor—for my mind! Last night I rushed around the house after preparing for my weekly Bible study and finally got everything together that I needed for class. I even fixed dinner for John before I dashed out to the car with only minutes to spare. I took a deep breath, reached into my purse for the car key—and suddenly my fingers sank into something soft and oily. You guessed it. A stick of *butter!* The one I had bought at the store the day before. The one I smuggled out of the grocery bag (before John unpacked it) and into my purse—and then promptly forgot about until now!

DEAR LORD, aren't we glad that *you* are our hiding place! We can run to you and be safe at any time. What comfort in the midst of all these senior moments.

I'll Get It

Dear God:

Did you hear the one about the three older women sitting around the kitchen table one morning? As they caught up on all their news—you know, kids, grandchildren, ailing husbands—the conversation suddenly shifted.

"I'm concerned," said Agnes. "There are times when I'll be standing at the bottom of the stairs with an armload of clothes and suddenly I can't remember if I'm taking them up to put away or bringing them down to launder them."

"I know what you mean," said her friend Milicent. "Sometimes I catch myself standing in front of the refrigerator with a jar of mustard in my hand and suddenly my mind goes blank. I can't for the life of me remember if I just took it out to put on my sandwich or if I'm putting it back."

Bertie, the third woman in the trio of friends, looked up and smiled smugly. "Well, I'm sure glad I don't have such problems," she said, then rapped her knuckles three times on the table for good luck. Seconds later, she stood up. "Someone's at the door," she announced. "I'll get it."

Good for a laugh! I'd like to think I'm not as absent-minded as Agnes or Milicent and not as proud and self-satisfied as Bertie. But the truth is there's a bit of all three of them in me. I can't deny it.

WITHOUT YOUR GRACE, I'd be a mess. But because of it, I'm the apple of your eye—no matter what I do or don't do. Thank you for loving me just as I am—a senior in transition!

Up Close and Personal

Dear God:

Last year many of my senior friends were wearing bifocals but I didn't have to—at least not yet, said the doctor. I could still see up close without my glasses. Yippee! Bifocals are for old people, I thought. (That's between you and me, Lord. I wouldn't say it out loud.)

But today in Sunday school class something seemed different. I couldn't read my notes with my glasses on, and I couldn't see the back of the room without them! Am I heading for the Land of Bifocals? Is it all downhill from here? No! I'm not ready for that.

I remember how I felt as I sat on the stool in front of my Senior Ladies' Bible Study. I was wearing my glasses at the time. Then when it was time to read the day's Scripture passage, I realized the print was too fine for me to read with my glasses on.

I took them off and laid them on the desk. "I have to take off my glasses to read," I said chuckling, knowing most of them have to put theirs on to read. As I picked up my Bible to lead the lesson, one of the ladies called out from the back of the room.

"That's okay, honey. You've got to do what you've got to do. Why, my uncle had to take out his teeth to eat!"

Suddenly I realized I was running my tongue over my teeth, checking for any loose parts! Bifocals, well, okay if I *have* to. But false teeth? No. I draw the line there!

LORD, ALL I REALLY NEED to be concerned with is doing "what is right and good" in *your* sight so it may go well with me (Dt 6:18).

Headphones and Casseroles

Dear God:

My parents are too funny! I wonder if I'm going to inherit their senior moments when I'm their age. This is one legacy I don't need! Give me their china or the Persian rug or the antique lamp or the handmade lace tablecloth, but please, not their senior moments.

It was my stepdad Ray's birthday, and I called Mom to see what he wanted or needed.

"I know he'd love a new headphone set," she said, "so he can listen to his ballgames."

I was thrilled. I had bought a set a year ago when it was on sale. It was still in the original package in my closet. I was just waiting for the right person and the right occasion to give it as a gift. I told Mom and she was pleased. She knew that Ray was considering buying one for himself. She would now suggest he put that on hold. Hint! Hint! "You never know what you *might* get for your birthday."

A couple of days later I spoke to Mom again. "What are you going to get Ray for his birthday?" she asked.

"Mom, we already had this conversation, remember? The headphones? The ones I bought on sale? You were delighted when I said I'd give them to Ray for his birthday."

"No way," she said. "You never said such a thing. I'd remember something that important."

The night of Ray's birthday I gave him the headphones. Mom continues to stick by her story that she never told me what to buy and that I never told her that I had purchased them the year before on sale.

Well, we got through that one. Whew! But, Lord, it didn't stop there, as you know. Remember when Ray called during the holidays to remind me to bring the infamous green bean casserole to our family Christmas dinner? I'm one of six kids and... You can see this one coming a mile away. He forgot who he told what to, so we all brought the same dish. We had enough green bean casserole to stretch into the following Christmas!

BUT AS SURE as I say this, your words come to mind: "Do not worry about your life, what you will *eat* or drink.... Is not life more important than food?" (Mt 6:25, emphasis added). Thanks for the reminder. My family is what matters—not the food we share.

Aleve Relief

Dear God:

What's a body to do to get some relief around here? My husband knows I have headaches among other ailments. All I need is a little sympathy and a couple of pain pills now and then. But even that appears to be too much for him. Last night I asked him to go upstairs and get me an Aleve. He took the longest time. I wondered if he had fallen asleep or fallen down.

Then I heard his footsteps on the stairs. He had a perplexed expression on his face—as though he wasn't sure what he had gone up for. He walked into the den, sat down in his favorite chair, and started watching TV, then stood up, went to the kitchen and poured a glass of water. How nice, I thought. He didn't forget after all. He's going to give me the pill and the water to take it with. I was really touched!

He came back to the den, sat down again, opened his clenched hand, looked at the pill, popped it in his mouth and chased it with a swig of water!

He appears to feel great.

Me? I still have my headache!

But I'm not alone—as I learned this morning after speaking with my friend. Last night she went to the medicine cabinet to get her husband a Tylenol PM and absentmindedly took it herself. "First I squealed with regret," she said, laughing, "then slept like a baby!"

THE BIBLE SAYS that a cheerful heart is good medicine (Prv 17:22). Now I really understand this truth. Laughter is even better than Aleve.

Tell It Again, Sam!

Dear God:

One thing about senior moments. We forget *them*, too! Last week during my husband's weekly Bible study for seniors we had a funny experience. Four of the people are over eighty, and the rest are at least seventy or more. Still, they are a lively group and very interested in studying the Word of God.

George wanted to grab their attention right away—before they nodded off, which occurs more often than he'd like. He cracked a joke about senior moments taking over his life and how even his own memory is a bit less sharp than it used to be.

Everyone laughed. He couldn't have asked for a better response. He must have felt very powerful at that moment. Not one person looked elsewhere.

When he finished, I leaned over to my husband and whispered in his ear. "Amazing," I said, as the students continued chuckling and talking among themselves. "You'd think they'd never heard that joke before."

"They haven't," my husband said, looking at me with a puzzled expression.

"You told it last week," I said. "Don't you remember?"

"I certainly do not," he replied with confidence.

It appeared the joke was on *me*, however, since I was the *only* one in the room who remembered it.

As I smiled to myself I was reminded of the exhortation from Proverbs 15:13: "A happy heart makes the face cheerful." So I joined in the laughter, then opened my Bible and settled down to the lesson, hoping he wouldn't repeat the same one we had studied the week before!

MAYBE WHAT WE both need to remember, Lord, is *your* teaching in Luke: "For the Holy Spirit will teach you at that time what you should say" (Lk 12:12). If we call upon your Spirit, instead of relying on our own recollection, we will not go wrong.

Grandma's Letter

Dear God:

Today I'm really feeling my age. So I pulled out this funny letter someone sent to give me a chuckle. I want to share it with you.

Dear Granddaughter:

One would think I'm a frivolous old gal from the looks of things. But actually I'm still a conservative grandmother who just happens to be in a relationship with five of the most unlikely gentlemen. As soon as I wake up, Will Power helps me get out of bed. Then I visit John. Charlie Horse comes along, and when he's here he takes a lot of my time and attention. When he leaves, Arthur Ritis shows up for the rest of the day. He doesn't like to stay in one place very long, so he takes me from joint to joint!

After such a busy day, I'm really tired. Ben Gay soothes my aches and pains so I can drift off to sleep. What a life! Oh, yes, Some people think I'm flirting with Al Zymer. But I'm not. I'm trying to keep him as far away as possible.

Love, Grandma

P.S. The preacher stopped by the other day. He said

at my age I should be thinking of the hereafter. "Oh, I do it all the time," I said. "No matter where I am—in the living room, in my bedroom, in the kitchen, in the den or basement—I ask myself, 'Now, what am I here after?'"

HERE ON EARTH I may not always know what I'm "here after," but one thing is certain. I know where I'm going after I die—to heaven to live eternally with you. I will not forget that!

AAADD

Dear God:

I thought you should be the first to know! I was recently diagnosed with AAADD (Age-Activated Attention Deficit Disorder). In case this is new to you, here's how it goes: I decide to do the laundry, start down the hall and notice the newspaper on the table.

"I'm going to do the laundry," I tell myself, "but *first* I'm going to read the newspaper."

After that I notice the mail on the table. Okay, I'll just put the newspaper in the recycle stack, but *first* I'll look through the pile of mail and see if there are any bills I need to pay. Yes! Now where is the checkbook? I wonder.

Look at that—the empty glass from yesterday on the coffee table.

Time to look for the checkbook, I chide myself. I have to get those bills in the mail by the due date. But *first*, I need to put the glass in the dishwasher.

I head for the kitchen, look out the window and notice my poor flowers need a drink of water, so I put the glass in the sink and head for the watering can—that is, until I notice the remote control for the TV is lying on the kitchen counter.

"What's it doing there?" I ask aloud—though I'm in the house alone! "I'll just put it away," I murmur, "but first I need to water those plants."

As I head for the door—aaagh! I step on the dog. Poor thing. He's hungry. Needs to be fed. Okay, I'll put the remote away, then water the plants—but *first* I'll feed the dog.

Suddenly it's dark outside. The day is over.

"Where did it go, Lord?"

The laundry is not done, newspapers are still on the floor, the glass is still in the sink, bills are still piled on the table, the checkbook is still lost, and the dog chewed on the remote control!

And when I try to figure out why I did not accomplish anything I set out to do, I'm completely baffled because as you know, Lord, you watched me—*I was busy all day!*

I realize my condition is *serious.* I need to get help, but *first,* I think I'll check my e-mail.

ON SECOND THOUGHT, what I really need to do first is check in with you. "Therefore I tell you, whatever you ask for in prayer, believe that you have received it, and it will be yours" (Mk 11:24).

Margarine, Margarine, Wherefore Art Thou?

Dear God:

Oh, for the good old days when my mind could run on a couple of tracks at once. Now that I'm a senior, it can't—or won't! You must have chuckled while watching me pack my lunch, fill my book bag and put the last touches on my hair, before going off to work, only to recall suddenly that I had laid a tub of margarine somewhere. But where? Remember me checking the bathroom, wondering if I'd set it down while picking up the can of hair spray?

I had wanted to take some margarine for my lunch. Oh, well, I thought, at least it's in a sealed container *somewhere*. Even if it's ninety degrees outside, it won't melt.

I never did locate it *that* day, but three days later, there it was in the drawer where I keep the lids of my plastic containers. It was soft—but not spoiled—just right for use in making cookies.

Apparently I mistook the whole container for a lid and tossed it in the drawer while hurrying to get ready for work. I even surprise myself, Lord, so I can only imagine how some of these "moments" look to you!

By the way, that batch of cookies turned out just right!

THANK YOU for loving me even when I'm forgetful, a bit foolish and when I can't find what I think I need.

Don't Forget to Remember

Dear God:

You saw me do it—just before I went to bed. I carefully noted on my calendar the department meeting scheduled for 10:30 A.M. on Friday, the thirteenth of July. I did not want to be late for this one. I had something to say to the committee, and I wanted to be there to say it myself!

I even laid out my clothes ahead of time so I wouldn't feel rushed the next morning. Then I took a leisurely bath, climbed into bed and drifted off to sleep.

I arose early the next day, and after prayers and coffee and toast and jam, I went right to work in the yard. Then I wrote a couple of letters and dashed off to the supermarket. Late in the afternoon I told myself, aloud, "Joan, *do not* forget the meeting tomorrow morning."

"Tomorrow? Wait," I scolded myself. "Tomorrow is today. I mean, look," I shouted as I glanced at the calendar on the wall. "*Today* is the thirteenth. I forgot the meeting. Maybe I'm wrong," I said, stalling. "How could I forget such an important thing? Not possible. Check the date on the computer. It isFriday, July 13, all right."

I felt like such a fool. It might as well have been April Fool's Day!

Alarmed, I phoned the lady in charge and expressed my

apologies. No excuses, just chagrin. How can one excuse a total lapse of memory? But she did and it was a welcome relief.

JUST AS JOB was "protected from the lash of the tongue" (Jb 5:21), you protected me from stinging words. She was gracious in reminding me that we all make mistakes sometimes.

She Loves Me, She Loves Me Not

Dear God:

What a kick! Today I heard a cute story about an elderly widow and widower who lived in a mobile home park in Florida. They had known each other for years and had become good friends. But each had a senior moment that nearly broke up their budding romance!

One evening during a community supper in the activity center, the two were seated across from each other at the same table. During the course of the meal, the man cast a few admiring glances at the woman. She returned his attention with shy smiles. Finally he gathered enough courage to ask her an important question. "Will you marry me?"

After a few seconds of careful consideration, she responded. "Yes. Yes, I will."

The meal ended with more pleasant exchanges. They said good night and each went home.

The next morning, the man awakened feeling troubled. "Did she say 'yes' or did she say 'no'?" he pondered aloud. "I can't recall!"

He didn't have even a faint memory of the woman's response. Embarrassed, he reached for the telephone and dialed her number. She answered and he quickly explained that he was no longer remembering things as well as he used to. He hoped she'd be patient with him. "I enjoyed our time together at the dinner," he said, "but one thing puzzles me. When I asked you to marry me, did you say, 'Yes,' or 'No'?"

"Why, I said, 'Yes, yes, I will,' and I meant it with all my heart," the woman replied. "And I am so glad you called," she continued, "because I couldn't remember who had asked me."

LORD, HOW LIKE these two I am sometimes. You ask me to do something, and I can't remember what it is—or do I intentionally forget? Or I hear you clearly and I simply ignore taking action until it's too late. Help me today to be attentive to what I say and what is said to me and to rely on you when I have a senior moment!

Here's the Parking Lot—
Now Where's My Car?

Dear God:

Talk about embarrassing moments—senior moments, panicky moments—this was one of them. I left the luncheon feeling like a million dollars. I made new friends, enjoyed a delicious meal, was inspired by the music, felt great about my presentation. Then it happened. I walked out the front door of the banquet hall with two other women, and I went blank. Absolutely *blank!* There in front of me was a sea of cars—but I had no idea where mine was located. I started walking and hoping and praying. Remember? I shouted to you in my mind, "Here's the parking lot. Now where's my car?"

If I'd been alone I'd have shouted out loud. But I couldn't lose my cool in front of these women. They were impressed with me—thought I was a celebrity! They wanted more of my books and my autograph. "Do you have any extras in your car?" one asked.

"Sure," I mumbled. "Authors always have extra books in their cars (now if I can just find my car). Why don't you wait right here?" I suggested. "I'll run to the car (if I can find it) and come back with the books signed and ready...."

"Oh, no," said one. "We'll follow you. No sense in your walking all the way back. Our car is in the lot, too."

Follow me? My hands were suddenly wet and my mind was numb. I wondered if they'd be so eager to follow me if they knew I was going in circles.

"Sure, right this way," I said, clearing my throat and blinking back tears. I didn't have a clue where I was heading. My trusted, faithful car, clean, dependable—and paid off—was nowhere to be seen.

"Help, Lord, I'm having a senior moment!" I called in my mind.

Then suddenly it all came back. Clear. Vivid. Certain. I had parked in the first lane by the exit on purpose—so I wouldn't get in a long line going out. Whew! In the nick of time you answered me. My honey of a car, gleaming in the sun from the fresh car wash, was right where I had left it—six cars to my right—practically in front of me. It never looked better. I wanted to wrap my arms around it, hug it, smooch it!

"Here we are," I chirped. "I'll get the books, sign them, and you can be off...."

The ladies smiled, scribbled out their checks, handed them to me, and off they went, thanking me as they waved good-bye.

I thanked them, too.

But *you're* the one who deserves the thanks, Lord, and the hug and the big smooch! Once more your Holy Spirit came to my rescue.

YOU ARE such an awesome God. You keep me from flying too high—where I might be tempted to believe I can handle things on my own. And you keep me from dipping so low that I despair. Instead, you keep me dependent on you—which is just where I need to be!

Spellbound

Dear God:

I can hardly believe what happened today in that third-grade Sunday school class. As a guest teacher, I was a bit nervous. I hoped the children would like me and learn something from the lesson. I was proud of myself for bringing along a flannel-graph and flannel cutouts to teach the story of Elijah. I was sure it would be a good way to capture attention and illustrate the points I wanted to make.

I was so relieved when I looked out at the boys' and girls' sweet faces. Everyone seemed spellbound! Their interest spurred me on.

Then suddenly one little boy looked at me intently and interrupted my teaching. "You're old, aren't you?" he asked.

I wasn't sure what to say. I guess to him—I am.

"I'm old enough to be your grandmother," I said, trying to make light of it.

"I don't think so," he said, frowning. "My grandma's *really* old," he said. "We had a party for her when she turned sixty."

Whew, Lord! I have five years to go before I look *really* old. What a relief! I won't doubt that I've entered a new season of life, but *old?* I'm not buying it. In some movie theaters and restaurants I don't even qualify yet for the "senior fare" or the "senior meal." I guess I could shrug it off. Maybe I should.

No. I'll tell the truth. I'm older, maybe not *old*, but older. I'm someone who is making the most of this time of my life—focusing on being kind, upbeat and mature. I want to be a woman who still has enough vim and vigor left to continue teaching, giving of myself to others and enjoying whatever opportunities you bring my way.

I KNOW THAT you count a gentle and quiet spirit to be of great worth (2 Pt 3:4). Help me to be such a person no matter what.

Beauty or the Beast

Dear God:

I know in your Word (1 Pt 3:3-5) you say that you want my adorning to be that of a holy woman who trusts in God. Makes me wonder what you think of my fourteen-carat gold earrings, my expensive haircut or my $30 nails. I want to have a meek and quiet spirit, but, Lord, do I have to be a *plain* holy woman?

Now that I'm a senior, however, these beautifying moments are turning into beautifying hours! I have to set my alarm for 6:00 A.M. if I want to make the 9:00 A.M. church service on Sunday—and church is only two blocks away!

After an hour or more in front of my bathroom mirror, as I try to get this aging face ready, I feel guilty. I guess I need to talk to you about this. I admit it! I depend on cosmetics when I want to look my best. All this "natural beauty" stuff doesn't work for women my age. I appreciate what you've given me, but let's be honest here, I'm not exactly glamorous. I work at it. And Revlon helps me out a lot (not to mention Playtex). As I look at the beauty products stacked on my vanity, I realize that beauty is a whole lot deeper than one's skin.

Probably, though, most people don't think about that. They're impressed by skin. I can imagine this gets to you sometimes! I mean, there is so much more to our bodily temples than what a person sees at first glance, and yet we put so much attention on the outside.

It's difficult to admit this, but I've gone to great lengths to make myself look young and beautiful, and some of it is pure *torture!* I've plucked my eyebrows, pierced my ears, teased my hair, shaved my legs, peeled my face, steamed my body and slept with pins and rollers on my head. I've endured starvation, aerobic exercise, smelly hair coloring, mud on my face, hot curling irons and loud hair dryers. I've put everything on my hair from mayonnaise to tin foil! At times, I must look like an alien from outer space.

The truth is, there aren't many "natural beauties." I *know!* I've been with women in salons, gyms, locker rooms and on camping trips. Where Estée Lauder ends, Maidenform begins. There are lots of products that create the illusion of youth and beauty. They can't be all bad. Can they?

I confess I've clogged my pores with eye shadow, foundation and miscellaneous contaminants, and after inhaling excessive amounts of hair spray and perfume, I've stuffed myself into tight pants, cinched my waist with belts and hung various rocks and metals around my neck. I carry a heavy bag on my shoulder, walk out of the house on stilts, all while trying to ignore the stiff wires that hold up a sagging bosom. I'm getting too old for all this!

I could write a book on beauty techniques. It has taken me countless hours to learn what I know about the subject. Things like I mustn't cream my hands before I floss my teeth, knowing it's a waste of time to curl my eyelashes before I say my prayers and that I should get out of bed in the morning while it's still dark.

The other day my husband caught me after I'd applied a

green anti-wrinkle facial mask and stuck an old shower cap over my hair. It's strange hearing a grown man scream! When he composed himself, I just smiled broadly, exposing the blue whitener on my teeth. "Look for my inner beauty, honey."

I trust that he does—and has—after forty-plus years of marriage!

I AM BLESSED to know that *you* always look past my skin to the depths of my heart and see me as your beautiful daughter.

Who's Who?

Dear God:

Here's a cute story that I just have to share with you. Maude was confined to a wheelchair, so she was very pleased one day when a gentleman resident asked her to join him for the nursing home's Sweethearts Banquet, where the king and queen for the next year would be elected.

Maude couldn't wait for this special evening. She asked a nurse's aide to help her prepare. The day of the banquet, the aide assisted Maude with her makeup, curled her hair and pulled it back with a beautiful bow, then zipped her into her finest dress—a shimmery pink gown trimmed in white lace.

"You must be so excited," the aide said, smiling, as the two looked at Maude's reflection in the long mirror in the hall.

Then without apparent reason, Maude burst into tears. The aide was taken by surprise. "Why this sudden change?" she asked. "You were so happy just moments ago."

No amount of questioning or comfort could stop Maude from sobbing. Finally, she caught her breath long enough to gasp, "I'm excited about going to the banquet, but I can't remember which gentleman asked me to go with him!"

A CUTE STORY that brings a chuckle on the one hand, but also causes me to think of your promise that the Holy Spirit helps us in our weakness—no matter what weakness it might be. Thank you, Lord, that when I forget who's who, you're there to supply the name.

Making the Rounds

Dear God:

As you know, our hospice has two therapy dogs on staff that visit patients in nursing homes. Our beautiful golden retriever, Andy, was the obvious favorite of a lady named Beatrice. Every time Andy made his rounds, Beatrice called to him, and Andy ran over to her and laid his head in her lap to be petted and scratched. It was obviously a mutual admiration society. I asked Beatrice why she preferred Andy over our other dog.

"Oh, he looks just like my poor dead husband," she said.

I'll never look at Andy the same way again!

This work is never without surprises, Lord. Recently, as you know, one of my hospice patients passed away, leaving her devoted husband devastated at her death. Since they both were residents of the assisted living facility where I have other patients, I stopped by to make a condolence call on the widower. Louis was appropriately tearful, acknowledging his grief and sadness at losing his beloved wife.

"You need to go on living," I counseled after he shared his memories, "and participate in the activities offered at the facility. In time, you'll begin to heal."

Louis was miles ahead of me. "Oh, I now belong to the ROMEO club," he said, slapping his knee and smiling broadly.

My face must have registered a bit of shock.

"I guess I need to explain," he said. "ROMEO stands for Retired Old Men Eating Out," he added with a swish of his hand.

Relief swept over me. I didn't want my imagination to take me any further!

I LIKED THINKING of Louis enjoying life to his heart's content, as you promised in Proverbs to those who are righteous in you.

Four Eyes

Dear God:

It's like this! If I could find a pair of glasses that didn't have to rest on my nose, I might be okay. But you know I'm one of those people who can't stand things like collars that rub against my neck, earrings that pull on my ears, and hats, helmets or hairpins. They drive me crazy.

I've gone all these years without glasses, and I'm grateful for that. The last few years have been tough, though. I've tried to put it off, but no longer. The eye doctor says I need glasses. He actually had the audacity to say that few people *"my age"* manage without them. Still, if you could give me a few more years of good eyesight, well, I'd appreciate it.

According to my friends, glasses are a big nuisance.

They're hard to keep clean. (Sounds like my kids when they were toddlers.)

The tiny screws come loose. (My son tells me I already have a few loose screws.)

They fog up when it's humid outside or when a person opens the oven door to check on the casserole.

And my friends complain that they can't see what they're doing when they try to clean or repair them.

One friend (who, just between you and me, is a little vain) moaned that along with the annoyance of wearing something across the primary part of her face, she found that glasses leave little dents on the side of her nose and hook into her hair. And although she likes to color-coordinate her outfits, it's impossible to have a pair of glasses for every dress and suit.

The pianist at my church grumbled that hers slip off her nose when she's playing during the offertory, or at home when she's baking cookies.

God, I hope you'll spare me these tribulations. Besides, I'm becoming forgetful lately. I can just see myself leaving them behind at the grocery checkout counter or in a restaurant or at the dentist's office.

It seems my early habits have done me in.

I never liked carrots!

I spent too many hours glued to the "tube."

I read books in too little light.

Looks like the jig is up. I'll be wearing glasses before the month is out. No more excuses. Remember when I went shopping a few weeks ago? I waved to my friend Marie standing just inside the front window of Macy's. I smiled and ran up to greet her—but when I got close, I suddenly realized I had been grinning at a mannequin, not Marie!

That night I called my husband to kill an insect in our pantry. "Insect?" he asked with a quizzical expression. "Honey, it's a *raisin*," he said and plopped it into the trash.

He insisted on driving me to the eye doctor. After the examination, I bumped into the door as I was leaving the office. Doc stuck his head out and quipped, "I'll put a rush order on those glasses, Connie."

I have to admit—I can't wait to pick them up.

MORE IMPORTANT, dear Lord, is that I see *you* more clearly—and for that I do not need prescription glasses, just a clean heart.

A Unique Dining Experience

Dear God:

For years Aunt Florence and seven of her elderly lady friends met each month to play bridge and have lunch together. I remember a time when it was Harriet's turn to host the event.

When the bridge game ended, she went into the kitchen to pour the beverages.

As the ladies talked, they moved over to the dining room table laden with bowls of delicious snacks. Mary and Helen each selected something and began to eat.

"This is an unusual slice of apple," Helen said.

Her friend Jewel tried another selection and thought it was dried bell peppers.

Then Florence tried a piece. "This is interesting—not much to it. Maybe it's beef jerky. What do you think, Mary?"

"Whatever it is, it's awful. Tastes like the bark of a tree," Mary whispered, making a face.

Helen decided to put her glasses on. Suddenly she chuckled out loud. "Look, ladies. No wonder it's so flat. This is potpourri!"

As Harriet returned with the drinks, everyone was in hysterics. "What's so funny?" she asked. "Did I miss something?"

"Oh, no," one answered, still laughing. "Just something Helen said."

Harriet never did find out that her friends were so hungry they resorted to potpourri for lunch. They decided to keep their senior moment a secret!

I'M GRATEFUL you're teaching me the secret of being content in any and every situation, whether I'm feeling confident or confused.

My Forgetter

Dear God:
Here's a cute poem by Esther Hollahan that speaks to all of us who have a growing number of senior moments. I'm enjoying it all over again as I write it here.

Seniors' Lament

My forgetter's getting better
But my rememberer is broke,
To you that may seem funny
But, to me, it is no joke.
For when I'm HERE I'm wondering
if I really should be THERE.
And when I try to think it through
I haven't got a prayer!
Oft times I walk into a room and say,
"Now, what am I here for?"
I wrack my brain, but all in vain
A zero is my score.
Oftimes I put something away,
where it is "safe", but, gee,
The person it is "safest" from
Is generally, ME.

When shopping I may meet someone,
Say, "Hi." and have a chat
Then, when the person walks away,
I ask myself, "Who's that?"
Yes, my forgetter's getting better
And my rememberer IS broke
And it's driving me plumb crazy
So it isn't any joke.

I'M BLESSED to know, dear God, that you, too, forget—all my sins—and remember them no more. But you *always* remind me of how much you love me—especially at times when I forget!

A Hair-Raising Experience

Dear God:

What's the difference between a senior moment and a "mental pause"? Maybe one leads to the other. That occurred to me during our recent trip.

Thank you for making it possible for us to have fun and to relax on our family vacation. The resort in Florida was beautiful. I felt so pampered, surrounded with big, fluffy towels and lovely bottles of scented lotion, shampoo, conditioner—mine to indulge in as I wished.

Each day I lathered my body generously with that aromatic potion in the green bottle. I had never before used anything as rich and fragrant. I wasn't sure what it was—but it didn't matter. It smelled *so* good. The print on the label was too tiny to read. I didn't need to know. It was a delicious experience, and I didn't want to interrupt my reverie by hunting for my reading glasses.

On our final day I decided to spruce up one last time before departing. I spread one of the rich lotions over my legs, then reached for my razor. Within seconds I knew something was terribly wrong! I grabbed my glasses and read the fine print on the label. The bottle I had selected was not shaving creme. It was hair conditioner—not recommended for shaving legs, unless they are very hairy!

When I shared this with my friends, one laughed out loud. She had had a similar experience the week before. "In the ladies' room at a restaurant," she said, "I noticed a collection of several spray cans in a basket on the counter."

"How nice of the management," I thought. "I must compliment the manager on the way out." I reached for a can as I primped my hair in the mirror. A touch of spray was all I needed to keep it in place a few more hours.

Spritz! Oh, no! As I set down the can I saw the word *Pledge* across the front. Too late! I was determined to make the best of a bad hair moment. I pushed open the door, walked out of the bathroom and into the restaurant with a head of hair that was as shiny as the coffee table in my living room and had the unmistakable scent of "lemon fresh" you-know-what.

I WAS A BIT ruffled at first, but then I took refuge in the remembrance that Mary Magdalene used pure nard—an expensive perfume—on your feet, oh Lord, and she wiped them with her hair. Surely she walked out of the house that day with a beautiful fragrance wafting behind her. A little nard. A little Pledge. No harm done!

Dairy Queens

Dear God:

What a cute story this is. My friend Carole's mother had a dear friend, Mary Elizabeth, who died recently. But while the woman was alive she and Carole's mom were the best of buddies. In later years they were both widows so they did everything together.

One day they went to Dairy Queen to order a new item they had seen advertised. They drove up to the drive-through window, and Mary Elizabeth, who was driving, said to the girl at the window, "We'd like two *Winds*."

"Winds?" asked the girl, appearing puzzled. "We don't have anything like that."

Mary Elizabeth was blown away at this reaction (and she didn't yet have the *wind* in her hand)! Clearly this employee was not up-to-date with the current ice cream menu.

"You know—the new item you advertised in the paper!" she said, her voice rising with impatience.

After a moment or two of discussion between them, the girl's eyes lit up. She suddenly *got* it! "Oh," she said, with a smile, "you want the new *Breeze.*"

LORD, OUR AMUSING ways must surely bring a smile to your face! Thank you for loving us when we are out of touch as well as when we are in sync.

Pay Up Or ...

Dear God:

How about these shop owners? Pretty shrewd when it comes to working with seniors. My husband and I had the same experience as an acquaintance. We each took a load of items to a local cleaner in different neighborhoods at different times. As we stepped up to the counter, the clerk asked for advance payment.

"That'll be $2.50 for the blouse, $9.00 for the suit, $4.00 for the sweater. Total comes to $15.50."

Upset by this new policy, I was determined to voice my disagreement.

"I'm reluctant to pay ahead of time," I stated firmly. "What if I'm not satisfied with the result? What recourse will I have? Everything is in *your* favor. You'll have my clothes *and* my money!"

The young man looked over the top of my head to the wall at the front of the store. "New owners. New policy, ma'am." (In other words, "take it or leave it.")

I decided to leave it. I gathered up my clothes and walked out.

"Well, I never," I told my husband. "That's the last they'll see of us."

My husband, the cool, calm, collected individual that he is, helped me simmer down as he related his analysis of this new business practice.

"The new owner," he said, with mock solemnity, "has likely deduced that in this community of seniors, if he waits for payment until services are rendered, he runs the risk that the customer (a) may not remember to pick up the cleaned items or (b) may die before the order is ready!"

We both laughed. There was probably more truth than fiction in his conclusion.

The incident reminded me of the ninety-year-old gentleman who would only purchase ripe bananas because he realized he might not live long enough for the green ones to ripen!

We drove off with our bundle of clothes (and our cash) and stopped for lunch where the waiter was eager to serve us first—and then accept payment. And we are alive to talk about it!

THANK YOU, Lord, that through you my days will be many, and years will be added to my life (Prv 9:11).

The Prodigal Partial

Dear God:

"Excuse me, have you seen my teeth? They were right here on the table with the silverware."

How's that for an opening line? My friend Janet had me smiling when she told me about her father, who actually removes his partial plate *just before eating!* One would imagine he needs it to eat, but no, he prefers to eat without it, so he slips it into his pocket or, worse yet, sets it down by his plate (unless he's with company).

He hates the thing, so he misplaces it more often than his wife cares to count. It isn't something one goes around telling people about, either—especially since it sometimes turns up in unexpected and unexplainable places, such as behind the refrigerator.

It's even been known to make it outside the familiar boundaries of the home front. Recently, while its owner was recovering from a mild stroke, his wife spent hours trying to locate the plate. She mentioned her frustrating search to the ladies at the antique store where she worked.

"Oh, is *this* it?" asked Shirley, the clerk, as she reached under the counter and pulled out a partial that looked mighty familiar.

Sure enough. Like the errant son in the Bible, the *prodigal partial*, once lost, had been found.

LORD, YOU ARE faithful to help us let go of what we cannot control.

I'm Here! But What For?

Dear God:

Thank you for coming to my rescue this morning. I entered the room full of administrators and suddenly there I stood, the coordinator of instructional support in a growing school district, and I didn't have a clue why we were meeting. "I'm here," I told myself, "but what for?" Remember how my heart raced and my hands shook?

How frightening! I knew every person there—so I'll give myself a point or two for that—but with such a cross-section of positions represented I could not remember why we all came together. Then I glanced at the folder on the table in front. It was labeled E.L.O. Again—a blank. I could imagine the facilitator looking me square in the eye and barking, "Ann, tell us, what are *you* doing here?"

A thought tumbled forward. "Check your calendar!" So I did. The letters E.L.O. were written across the page in giant print. No help there!

I stopped for a moment. If I concentrate real hard I can usually pull the answer I need. E.L.O. How difficult can it be? I tried to squeeze the words out of my mind like juice from a dried up orange. Let's see ... Educational Lamebrain Organization or Elderly Looking Overwrought, or ...

I rifled through the notes in the folder. "It has to be here somewhere," I scolded myself. "I remember this group from another time. But what could we be meeting about today?"

I prodded my mind, waiting for it to toss me a clue. Most of us don't even work in the same department, I thought. Was this an employee picnic? A staff potluck? Then I felt worse. I didn't remember if I was supposed to bring something or not, and if so, what that might be. Was I on a committee and now everyone was angry with me? Another minute of this and I'd be rushing off to the ladies' room.

Suddenly everyone fell silent.

"Welcome to E.L.O." The presiding figure called the meeting to order. More agony. E.L.O. *E.L.O.!* Come on, someone, anyone—spit it out! I thought.

Then finally I heard the words I had longed to hear: *Extended Learning Opportunity*. Still—*why* were we together?

I glanced inside the file once again and there it was—the answer to my dilemma—a calendar for June, July and August. Then it dawned on me. *Summer school. In-service trainings. Opportunities for more learning.* Of course! I wanted to stand up and cheer. "Look, everyone. I'm here. And best of all, I know *why* I'm here! Count me in as an upstanding member of ... oh, never mind!"

LORD, YOU'VE TOLD me to cast all my anxieties on you because you care for me. I'm so grateful I can do just that. With you every opportunity is one of extended learning—and grace!

Moments We'd Rather Forget

Lean not on your own understanding; in all your ways acknowledge him.

PROVERBS 3:5-6

Trash on Rye—And a Side of Fries

Dear God:

Remember when I drove Mom and my stepdad, Paul, to the excursion boat in Louisville, Kentucky? We didn't know if a meal would be served while cruising, so on the way we stopped at Burger Barn to grab a bite to eat before boarding.

Mom and Dad are *more* senior than I am—yet *I* had the senior moment!

We pulled up to the drive-through station and waited our turn to call in our order. Then we chatted while waiting for someone—anyone—to acknowledge our presence so we could call out our meal choices. After several minutes with no service, I was growing impatient. And I was conscious of the time crunch. I didn't want us to miss the boat!

I noticed my stepdad glance out the window and then back at me with a curious expression on his face. "Cindy," he asked, "is there any reason why you've stopped in front of the dumpster?"

I looked out and, sure enough, we were parked by the trash bin.

I was mortified. How could I have done such a thing? It was so obvious—once Paul pointed it out to me, that is.

"Just checking ... um, you know, where to put our garbage—after we eat," I stammered.

Too late for excuses. Paul and Mom weren't buying it. It was *their* turn to watch me! And clearly they were enjoying it.

We all laughed as I moved the car forward to the station clearly marked: PLACE ORDER HERE. When our burgers and fries arrived, we ate quickly, then hurried to the boat dock, still giggling about my lunchtime antic—my senior moment at age forty-three.

AT TIMES LIKE THIS, Lord, I see my pride. I don't like being wrong, looking foolish, having someone point out a weakness. But it's also an opportunity for me to lighten up and laugh at my mistakes. Thank you for reminding me that I'm a human being after all.

It's Here Somewhere

Dear God:

Sometimes I wonder if walking doesn't beat driving any day. You and the disciples seemed to do just fine going from town to town on foot. You didn't have to make a car payment, keep track of bus tokens, wait for a train or put up with smog, flat tires and outrageous gas prices.

Enough grumbling! It is kind of funny, though, how quickly we humans get accustomed to our "chariots," whether a simple two-door with hand locks or a Lincoln Navigator that takes up a half block of parking space.

But I surrender. I'm as dependent on my car as anyone. So it really got my heart racing when I had just paid hundreds of dollars for an annual tune-up only to discover two days later that I still had a problem. The car was making an unusual sound every time I stopped at a traffic light. Something was clearly wrong with the idle that hadn't shown up during the test drive.

As soon as I arrived home after running errands, I called the auto repair shop and complained.

"Can you come in tomorrow?" the scheduler asked.

"I'll be there," I replied. Then I realized I'd need to show the work order and paid receipt to make certain I wasn't charged a second time.

"Where is that paper?" I questioned myself.

I looked in the glove box in the car. Then in the trunk and under the seats. Not anywhere that I could see. I searched my receipt file at home. No dice. "Think, woman. Think," I demanded. "You just had it two days ago."

I was about to give up. Then something pink caught my attention. I glanced at the calendar hanging on the wall above the telephone in the kitchen. You guessed it, Lord. (Actually, you knew all the time!) There was the work order and the receipt stapled to it—in full view—clipped to the calendar— so I wouldn't forget where I had put it!

THANK YOU FOR keeping your promise to lead me along straight paths—right where I need to go (Prv 4:11).

Super Sale!

Dear God:

What a moment! One I'd surely like to forget. I should have picked up my granddaughter from the school open house as my daughter asked me to—and gone straight home. I could have shopped another day—when I had my wits about me. But no, I thought it would be fun—and helpful—to take Lindsey along. Turns out I needed her more than I expected—or even wanted.

We had stopped in Robinson-May's lingerie department—just to look. But when I saw the sign SUPER SALE, I couldn't resist. I needed a couple of new bras. And the price was right. I thought we'd be in and out in a matter of minutes. How embarrassing to realize that it took over three hours to accomplish this simple mission. My daughter was worried. She couldn't reach us and she must have wondered what I had gotten into—and with Lindsey along, to boot.

I doubt Lindsey will ever want to shop with me again. I couldn't find what I was looking for. They no longer make the style I'm used to. And none of the other brands fit right. I spent three hours putting bras on and taking them off till I didn't know one from another. And poor Lindsey! She chased back and forth to the dressing room, bringing me assorted styles and sizes.

But the moment I *really* want to forget occurred when I handed the sales clerk the mound of bras I had tried on—my old one included! I'd have gone home without a bra if it hadn't been for Lindsey, who ran after the clerk and retrieved it.

Now that I've gotten that off my chest (no pun intended), help me move on, Lord. That senior moment is simply not funny—to me! I won't ask Lindsey or her mother what they think!

But still I have to laugh—when I think of it now.

LORD, I'M GRATEFUL for the ability to laugh at myself—especially when I'm embarrassed.

Can Do

Dear God:

What's happening to me? I open the refrigerator, and I can't remember if I'm putting something in or taking it out. If we had stairs I'd probably wonder if I was going up or coming down.

Remember the day I reached for my home-canned pine-apple juice from the pantry shelf? I could almost taste it! I added the golden liquid to the orange and lemon juice already in the pitcher in the fridge, and stirred it briskly.

Then I took a tall glass down from the cabinet, added crushed ice and poured the juice up to the top. Mmmm! The perfect refreshment on a hot afternoon. I raised the glass to my lips and took a long swig!

Ugh! It tasted strange, a bit oily, even salty. I smelled the remaining contents of the can. "Oh, no! Chicken broth!" I yelled.

That settles it. From now on I need to label all my cans and jars.

How silly of me—and what a waste. But, God, in your Word you say we should forget the things which are behind us.

Please help me forget past mistakes, sins that are forgiven, and the memory of actions that could hinder my spiritual progress. You also remind us in the Bible not to forget you and your blessings.

I WANT TO remember what I should not forget, and forget what I should not remember. With you all things are possible—even what appears to be impossible. By your grace and guidance I can do all things! Now for that cool glass of pine-apple juice. I labeled the pitcher this time!

Pie Soup

Dear God:

Friday was my daughter-in-law Grace's birthday. We planned to treat her family to dinner at a restaurant and then return to their house, play a board game and celebrate with a chocolate-cream freezer pie that I had prepared for the occasion. Since I wouldn't finish work until 6:00 P.M., I dropped off the dessert at her place that afternoon.

We met Grace, her husband Les and our granddaughter Laura at 6:30 and enjoyed a wonderful meal, then drove to their house. We were still too full to have dessert, so we started the game. I was keeping track of the time because I knew the pie had to be removed from the freezer about 20 minutes before serving or it would be too frozen to eat. At the proper time, I asked Laura to take it out and set it on the counter.

She returned with a puzzled look on her face. "Grandma," she asked, "is the pie supposed to be soupy? I didn't see it in the freezer so I checked the fridge."

Oh, no! At that moment I realized that in my hurry earlier that day I had put the pie into the refrigerator instead of the freezer. I confessed my senior moment and we all had a good laugh. I got up immediately and put the pie into the freezer and promised everyone we would enjoy it the next day—and we did.

HOW BLESSED I am that you are a God of second and third and fourth chances—and more. With you to guide and guard me, even mistakes can become opportunities.

He Deserves a Good Belt!

Dear God:

You told me to slow down—and of course, you were right. Aren't you always? I take it you enjoy a good laugh as much as anyone—or you wouldn't have let me make a fool of myself on Bob's birthday. That's what I get for rushing around—trying to do too many things in too short a time frame.

Remember how when I married him I thought it was great that Father's Day and his birthday were close together—about two weeks apart? I figured when we had kids it would be easy to take care of both occasions with one big party—and one big gift! Up to now, I've hit the target every time. I bought him just the right luggage, the golf clubs he wanted, the cashmere sweater he saw at Nordstroms. I was on a winning streak!

This year I thought I'd make things really special. And I was sure you'd approve, dear Lord. He's a senior now and I wanted to pamper him a bit. Two occasions. Two gifts. I was feeling quite proud of myself as I looked through his drawers (no pun intended) to find out what I could buy him. "A good belt! That's what he needs," I told myself. He hadn't owned a genuine leather belt in years.

My search was successful. I was able to find a stunning belt of good quality leather that I knew he'd like. On Father's Day he was obviously pleased.

"Honey, the belt is beautiful," he said and gave me a big hug. "I'm going to put it on right now."

I could tell he appreciated that I had spent more than usual on his gift as a way of honoring him on Dad's Day.

Then two weeks later, just before his birthday, I headed to the department store again. I was truly excited about finding another gift that had Bob's name all over it. Success! I rushed home, wrapped the gift in beautiful foil paper, finished it off with a giant red bow and a card that told him how much he meant to me. I couldn't wait for him to open the box. I knew I had found something he not only needed but would enjoy wearing. I stood by as he ripped open his package. Then he took my hand and looked at me with a bewildered expression.

"Honey, this is nice, but you just gave me a brown belt for Father's Day."

"*Really!*" I exclaimed, then slunk out of the room to cut the cake.

LORD, WHAT CAN I say? Except, "I goofed!" I hope he doesn't think any less of me for having this senior moment. I know you don't!

Squash That Bug!

Dear God:

I was so glad to talk with my friend Edie. She helped me gain some perspective on this scary thing called "floaters and flashes." I didn't even know the meaning of those words till I had my latest eye exam. In fact, I was feeling rather proud of my excellent eye health. Remember when the ophthalmologist told me last year that I had wonderfully healthy eyes for someone over sixty? I left his office feeling like a million dollars.

Then one day all that changed. I walked into my daughter's house and suddenly my left eye flashed crescent moons of light every time I blinked. At first I thought it was a reaction to the lime green paint on the walls in the den, but that night the same thing occurred. Bright flashes against the darkness spooked me. What was happening?

I had another thorough eye exam, and the doctor explained that as part of the aging process, the vitreous gel behind the eye begins to pull on the retina, causing flashing lights or lightning streaks such as I was experiencing. And I also noticed something called "floaters"—tiny clumps of gel or cells inside the eye that look like small specks or clouds moving in one's field of vision as they cast shadows on the retina. Floaters and flashes, I learned, could lead to retinal detachment. Scary stuff to hear about after so many years of excellent eye health.

After the exam, I was relieved to hear my retina had not torn—but the doctor also cautioned me to report any new developments. I went home sobered by the sudden change.

Edie lightened my load by sharing an experience of her own. One night as she and her husband were getting ready for bed, she saw an insect crawling up the wall.

"There's a bug," she called to Chuck. "Quick, get it."

He grabbed the fly swatter and went after the little beast but couldn't find it. "I don't see anything," he said. "It must have flown off."

Edie looked again and there it was—going up the wall just as before. "It's right there," she shouted while pointing in front of her. "Get it!"

Her husband still did not see a thing. Edie then noticed that the "bug" kept moving in the same direction as her eye.

"Oh, Chuck," she said, realizing what was going on, "it's not a bug after all. It's a 'floater' in my eye!"

"Chuck put down the fly swatter," she said, "and we both fell on the bed laughing at my senior moment."

LORD, PLEASE GIVE ME the eyes to see—not only a bug on the wall—but your Spirit at work in my life.

Good Ol' What's 'er Name

Dear God:

How can I remember the name of my fourth-grade teacher—Sister Mary Pius—but forget the name of my next-door neighbor or a person I met only moments before? I've heard all the tricks: Focus on the individual as you're introduced. Find something about the person to associate the name with, such as hair color or mannerism: Rosemary, the redhead, or Minnie from Minnesota. Repeat his or her name silently in your mind three times. "Lois, Lois, Lois." I tried that, but the name *Lois* wouldn't stick because the woman reminded me of my childhood playmate, Lucy Perkins! I kept saying, "Lucy, Lucy, Lucy," until I slipped and said it out loud.

Then there's the old use-the-name-in-a-sentence trick as soon as you hear the person's name. But it doesn't work for me. "It's nice to meet you, Redhead, I mean Rosemary." People look at me like I'm one taco short of a Mexican Special!

Fortunately, I've discovered I'm not alone. For example, did you hear the story about the two women playing bridge? They had known each other for years, lived in the same town and their kids grew up with one another. They had served on the same church committees and belonged to various civic organizations together.

Then one afternoon after years of playing bridge as partners, one looked across the table at the other and suddenly went blank. Her face flushed and she fidgeted with her cards, appearing to delay the next move. She wanted to say something to her partner, but then realized the woman's name had slipped her mind. Gone. Just like that. No use pretending, she decided silently. I'll have to ask. Surely she'll understand. She's my best friend.

"I'm so sorry," she said sheepishly, "but I can't remember your name. Isn't that awful? After all these years. Please, tell me. I can't stand the suspense."

Her partner looked across the table, staring into her eyes with a mix of hurt and anger. The first woman felt even worse. She couldn't imagine how she could repair this sudden breach in their relationship. Just as she was about to apologize—*again*—her partner looked up, smiled and said with a twinkle in her eye, "How soon do you need to know?"

OH LORD, THANK YOU for the gift of good friends and their patience. May I express the same toward them.

White-Knuckle Ride

Dear God:

I'm so pleased you have given me a heart's desire to lead women's groups to England on a tour of tearooms. The ladies enjoy this so much, and I delight in seeing their faces and hearing their reactions.

I like the fact that most of the women are middle-aged and older. They seem to be at a point in life when they have time to appreciate the lovely British tradition of high tea.

They also enjoy a tour of London in one of those famous double-decker buses. I'm chuckling as I remember the first group I took. None of the ladies had been to England before. What happened during that tour was my fault in a way. I realize I didn't spend enough time going over the instructions. Now that I'm planning another trip I must remedy that oversight.

As we boarded the bus that fine afternoon, most of the women decided to sit downstairs, out of the damp weather, but a few decided to sit on the top deck. I split my time between both so neither group would feel left out.

When I walked up the stairs to speak to those on the upper deck, I noticed my passengers were sitting like soldiers on alert. Not a word was spoken, and most of them clutched the seats in front of them. It appeared to be a white-knuckle ride!

"Is anything wrong?" I asked. "We're having a great time downstairs, but you don't appear to be very happy."

One of the ladies looked up at me with a touch of fear in her eyes. "Well," she said, in a small voice, "that's because *you* have a driver!"

LORD, THAT INCIDENT brings a chuckle, yet I can relate to that woman's fear. Sometimes it does feel as though I'm going through life without a driver. But that's only when I take my attention off you—the one who leads and guides—whether or not I'm aware in the moment. Thank you for taking care of me—no matter what.

Not a Moment Too Soon

Dear God:

I still have a couple of years to go till I can get a senior discount at the movies and till I qualify for the Golden Age Passport at national parks. But I'm having senior moments nonetheless. My older friends say it's normal. So I'll take their word for it. Remember the other day? It happened right in front of my very eyes (and yours, too).

I needed to pick up some groceries. So I perused the ads, matched my coupons, clipped them to my list, dug out my wallet to make sure I had enough cash, then headed for the store.

I got just about everything on my long list. I was so pleased. No extra trips necessary this week. I walked to the checkout stand, and the clerk rang up my total while her assistant bagged the food.

I reached into my purse for the money to pay. My wallet ... where was it? My heart pounded as I moved my hands frantically from one compartment to the next. Gone. My wallet was missing. There I stood—holding up the line, cash-poor and totally embarrassed. Then I realized I couldn't even drive home to get the money—because my driver's license was in my wallet. I had driven to the store without it. My mind had a field day. I could imagine the police waiting to nab me the moment I walked into the parking lot.

"Pull yourself together," I begged silently. "You're simply having one of those moments—the kind *seniors* have!"

The clerk put my bags aside while I stepped out of the aisle, called home, and thankfully, my sixteen-year-old son answered. He had a learner's permit. Of course he was thrilled to be able to rescue his mother by driving to the store to pick me up. Yes, my wallet was sitting on the kitchen table where I had left it. I was relieved to hear that.

Then I realized Dan couldn't drive without an adult in the car with him. I told him to call Grandma to accompany him. I took a deep breath, got over my embarrassment and realized why more women at midlife don't have babies. They'd set them on the floor and forget about them! I can handle misplacing my wallet—but not my kids.

THANK YOU for my children, Lord. They sure come in handy when I'm in a jam!

Water, Water Everywhere

Dear God:

I'm no plumber, but I know a leak when I see one. Today while putting back our clean towels in the cabinet under the sink in the bathroom (where my husband shaves), I noticed a puddle of water right in the middle of two stacks of towels. I turned on the faucet, then looked under the sink again, and sure enough, drip, drip, drip.

I showed my husband the spot that was leaking.

"Can you fix this," I asked, "or should I call a plumber?"

"I'll take a look," he said. "First I have to remove the pipe, so it will be a while before I get to it."

I knew that could mean days or even weeks. So I placed an empty pot on the cabinet floor to catch the water. "At least the towels will stay dry," I thought.

A few days later I ran another load of wash. Later, while stacking the fresh towels under the sink, I noticed the pot was about to overflow with the collected water.

I was a bit annoyed that my husband had not yet started the repair work and even more annoyed that he had not at least emptied the pot every few hours. "You would think ... he would at least ... check it," I said while bending over and carefully removing the pot. One false move and the water would have soaked the entire room.

"I'll empty this thing right now," I said to myself. "No sense in taking it all the way to the kitchen. I'll dump it into the sink ... no, not the sink," I yelled, catching myself too late, as the water poured right back into the cabinet and spilled onto the floor!

LORD, WAS THAT one of those senior moments I've been hearing so much about? P-l-e-a-s-e ... I'm too young for this!

Drink Up

Dear God:

I'm feeling the age difference between myself and my grand-daughter—to be sure. At eighty-three I'm told I'm spry as ever physically—even mentally—*most* of the time. But there are those "moments," the ones I'd rather forget. Just this week I told her I couldn't walk my usual four miles as quickly as I'd like. I tire more easily these days. Hate to admit it.

Kristi suggested I start taking ginkgo biloba capsules twice a day with a full glass of water. Apparently it helps one's memory. A couple of days after our discussion Kristi asked how I was feeling since I started the ginkgo. I had to tell the truth—even though I knew she'd be disappointed.

"I stopped," I said flatly, "because I *already* drink eight glasses of water each day, and if I take these pills I'd have to drink two more. I just couldn't drink all that..."

Then suddenly it hit me as my voice trailed off. I was having a *major* senior moment. She laughed, then I laughed. Well, Lord, I'm on the ginkgo again—only *this* time twice a day with two of the eight glasses of water I'm already drinking! I've certainly proved to myself and to my granddaughter that if ginkgo biloba improves one's memory, then I'm a prime candidate!

And so is my friend! While planning a visit to her son's home, she decided to take all her vitamins out of their bottles and put them in plastic bags to save space in her suitcase. No chance of mixing them up since she knew which ones to take once a day and which ones to take three times a day.

"For some reason," said my friend, "I also decided to put the vitamins I'd be leaving behind in pretty little glasses on the shelf. Then I threw away the bottles. When I returned from Iowa I put the surplus vitamins in the proper glasses. No problem."

No problem, that is, until one morning in July when she blanked out while assembling her vitamins for the day. She couldn't, for the life of her, remember which ones were in the small pink glass on the shelf. The supply had dwindled so she knew she had been taking the capsules for *something.* But what? She could remember all the others—but not that one. She was about to take a sample to the pharmacy or call her physician or stop by the health store—anything to solve this annoying mystery.

"Then," she said, "suddenly it occurred to me. The unknown vitamin was ginkgo biloba—which I had been taking to improve my memory. What a relief to know that it worked!"

LORD, I DON'T really need to worry, though, for your Spirit has promised to teach me all things and to remind me of what you have taught.

Zip It Up

Dear God:

Remember the day just before retirement when I was finishing my stint in the corporate library? The librarian and I each had our own cubicle. Mine was in the corner. Hers was in front of mine and behind the circulation desk. That day I was especially appreciative of the privacy because I felt so sick. My stomach had been bothering me for days. I could barely stay at my computer. I finally realized that if I loosened my skirt I could sit for longer periods more comfortably. Fortunately the skirt I was wearing that day had a zipper in front and a one-button waistband.

That morning the librarian asked me to look at something on her computer. I jumped up and walked quickly from my cubicle toward hers. By the time I got to her doorway, my skirt lay on the floor around my ankles! We both gasped in surprise, then burst out laughing. I yanked up my skirt and scurried back to my cubicle. Fortunately, no one else was in the library to witness my senior moment!

PROVERBS 31:25 says, "She is clothed with strength and dignity; she can laugh at the days to come." Amen to that!

A Sleeper If There Ever Was One

Dear God:

These senior moments are really getting to me! I woke up later than usual this morning and dashed out to church feeling a bit thrown together. When I arrived I ran into the ladies' room to touch up my hair and check my makeup. As I took a final glance in the full-length mirror, I was shocked to see the hem of my nightgown hanging below my skirt. I wondered how many people had noticed before I did!

I slipped into a stall and did a quick change, stuffing the pink nightie into my purse and hoping no one had seen me.

I remember at age twenty thinking it was fun to do such a thing. My college dorm mates and I used to sleep in on Sunday mornings till the last possible moment, and then jump out of bed and put on our choir robes over our pj's. We got away with it for about a year till the student in charge of our floor reported us to the dorm supervisor.

But that was then—and this is now—some forty years later. It's not funny anymore. In fact, it's downright scary. I wonder how many times I've done that before. I can just see it now—the lead story in the *Senior Gazette*.

WOMAN SHOWS UP AT
CHURCH IN NIGHTGOWN
Plans to Sleep Through Sermon?

PLEASE, GOD, not that. I've always wanted to be a headliner, but not at church and certainly not in my pink nightgown!

Your Name Is?

Dear God:

I'm glad I can share this with you. I picked up the phone yesterday and dialed.

"Hello." Someone was on the other end, but at the moment I didn't know who it was. I couldn't for the life of me remember who I was calling.

"Who's this?" I asked in a sheepish voice.

"Paula," the woman responded.

"Paula who?" I asked.

"Mom, this is Paula, your daughter!"

"Paula? Oh, I'm so sorry. I know it sounds silly," I said apologizing, "but I couldn't remember who I called!"

We had a good laugh—though I have a hunch I'll never live it down. She won't let me!

Oh, well. I'll just console myself with a couple of caramels. Better not. I was just informed by a friend who learned the hard way that sticky candy can pull off gold crowns.

Getting older really does have its low points! I can't even forget my troubles without damaging my teeth.

BUT THEN I think about living eternally with you in heaven, with my new body, and I won't have to be concerned with teeth or forgetfulness or senior moments!

Something to H-AARP About

Dear God:

My parents led the way. Gradually friends and neighbors followed. I watched from the sideline. I felt smug! I had at least ten more years before anyone could label me senior. While they all lined up for movie and clothing and restaurant discounts, I paid full fare and I was proud of it. Okay, I needed reading glasses at age forty-three, but I could still walk and run and button my own shirts.

"Ten percent here. Twenty percent there. It all adds up," said one. "Why pay full price when you don't have to?"

"What? Are they nuts?" I often thought. "I have my pride. I'll pay the extra dollar for a hamburger. I'll stand in line for the movies. I'm glad to pay full admission to enter national parks."

I'm too young for a curly perm and long-sleeved shirts! I'm too young to yawn my way through *Larry King Live*. I'm too young to even know the meaning of the phrase "senior moment."

Then suddenly it was the year of my forty-fourth birthday, and I was now aware of every joint and muscle in my body. Even though I had already heard a doctor say things like "early signs of this" and "early signs of that," I was still having fun!

My children were grown and gone, my lifelong dream

career was taking off, I was exercising regularly again and my husband and I were settling into our "empty nest" with regular dates and quiet evenings. It felt great to be alive!

Then, the day before my birthday, my husband walked in with the mail. The grin on his face indicated that something was up and probably up to no good! With a quick move of his hand, he flipped an envelope addressed to me onto the counter near where I was standing. I stared at the return address in amazement—no—shock. Addressed to me? Why me? A birthday card? No. A check from a recent speaking engagement? No. It was an invitation—to join AARP (American Association of Retired People).

Oh, no, I thought. It's all downhill from here.

UNTIL I REALIZED, Lord, there's no mention of retirement in the Bible. Shall I send a copy of *your* book to the AARP?

A Rose by Any Other Name ...

Dear God:

As you know so well, I've taught school for years and have always prided myself on learning the first and last name of over one hundred students the first week of school.

If only that would carry over to the rest of the people in my life. Alas! It has not. Yesterday I went outside to water my plants and saw my friend and neighbor busy doing the same thing in her front yard. I waved to her and called her by name.

About fifteen minutes later, I wanted to show her something in my garden. I walked across the street to her house, stood in the driveway and realized I could not remember her name—even though I had just said it moments before.

This is ridiculous, I scolded myself silently as my heart pounded. I was certain my face had turned red. I couldn't possibly admit that I had lost her name in such a short time. I mean, come on. We had carpooled to four graduate classes, helped one another with projects of mutual interest, eaten out together and so on. I was so stunned by my memory lapse that I just stood there.

Then I got down to business—serious business. I ran through a mental list of different female names to see if the right one would pop up. Joan, Ann, Martha, Linda, Sonja, Maria. It didn't help. I could not bring myself to walk up to her doorbell and ring it. It was just too much! What would she think of me? Suddenly she appeared at the door, greeted me by name, and I then—thank you, Lord—remembered hers, Marlene.

How does this happen? I can pull up the name of the kid who sat across from me in fourth grade—Stuart McCabe. I even can remember my first grade teacher's name—Mrs. Malinowski—for heaven's sake. Where is that stored? But the name of my neighbor and friend? Gone in seconds.

As soon as I got home I plastered the name MARLENE in big letters across my bulletin board so I'd never forget again. And then I decided to buy a jumbo-size board—just in case!

One consolation, dear God, is that I never need worry about forgetting your name. You have so many: Savior, Redeemer, Lord, Almighty God, Wonderful Counselor, Prince of Peace, Son of God, Jesus Christ, Holy Spirit.

NAME ABOVE ALL NAMES, be with me in these moments of forgetfulness when in my humanity I am reminded to cast all my cares on you, for you do care for me.

Big Foot

Dear God:

Today the very thing I thought would never happen to me—happened! You must have been smiling as you observed my predicament.

"Could you hold this for me?" I asked my husband as I handed him my shopping bag and headed toward the ladies' restroom at the factory outlet mall. I pushed open the heavy door and made a beeline for the only stall in sight. How odd, I thought. In a huge crowded place like this, you'd think they'd have more than one stall. Women always have to wait in line because of this kind of stupid planning—probably by a committee of men!

Oh, well, no use getting upset. At least there's no line. I'll be in and out in a jiffy. As I situated myself and hummed a little tune, I heard the restroom door open, then slam shut. Next the sound of running water penetrated the stillness.

I glanced through the space between the bottom of the stall and the floor and saw the lower half of two denim-clad legs. My gosh, that lady has big feet, I thought, as my gaze traveled downward to the bulky white sneakers she wore.

I finished up and pushed open the stall door. Then my heart dropped into *my* shoes as I laid eyes on a twenty-something gentleman who appeared as shocked to see me as I was to see him.

"Uh-oh," I stammered weakly, "I guess I'm in the wrong restroom." I rushed out, trying to catch my breath, as I barreled back to where I had left my husband moments before. My face was still on fire when I reached him.

"Are you okay?" he asked. No doubt he noticed my stricken expression.

"I'm f-f-fine," I answered, not ready to explain my senior moment. "I just saw. ... I saw *Big Foot!*"

"You saw *what?*" my husband asked.

"Oh, never mind," I squeaked. "Let's grab some lunch. I'm feeling a bit light-headed."

HOW DIFFICULT it is to admit my mistakes to my family and friends, particularly when I'm ashamed and embarrassed. But *you* know the whole truth about me, so I can always come to you.

Click, Click!

Dear God:

Here's a cute one about my friend's parents. Bill and Jane awakened one Saturday morning and decided to go to Perkins Cafe for breakfast. After eating, Jane excused herself and went to the ladies' room. Bill waited at the table, then decided he'd make a similar stop. He walked into a little stall and shut the door when suddenly he heard the click, click of high-heeled shoes on the tiled floor.

Oh, no! he thought, a woman had gone into the men's bathroom by mistake. He decided to wait it out. She'd be finished in a minute and then he could slip out with no one the wiser. At last he heard the retreating click, click of her heels and the whoosh of the door as the woman walked out.

Bill was aware that someone else was holding out in the stall next to him. He assumed that man had similar thoughts to his own. Being the friendly type, he called out, "Did you hear that? There was a woman in here. Lucky for her she didn't see either one of us, or she'd have been mighty embarrassed!"

"Bill, is that you? What are *you* doing in the women's bathroom?" Jane called in a loud whisper.

"I'm having a senior moment," he replied weakly, then beat it out the door without looking back or listening for any more clicking heels!

LORD, THAT MUST have been quite a sight. Mercifully, it was his wife, not another woman, who discovered his mistake. I'm sure he thanked you for bailing him out—once again.

Free for the Taking

Dear God:

I put things in a safe place, an easy-to-find place, a place I can't possibly forget—and then I do.

Last Saturday, my husband and I had tickets for a local concert, but then suddenly we decided to go out of town. I hated to see the tickets go unused so I called a music-loving friend and asked if she'd like them. She was delighted.

"I'll leave them in my mailbox by the road," I told her.

"Great. I'll be by to pick them up later today," she responded.

My husband and I went off for the weekend and had a restful, relaxing time. On Saturday night I envisioned my friend sitting in our front-and-center seats enjoying the concert. I was so glad I had thought to ask her. She was the one friend who would truly appreciate such an unexpected (and free) treat.

On Sunday we attended a worship service at a local church. During the sermon I opened my handbag to take out a tissue. I gasped in disbelief. There were the concert tickets sticking out of a small pocket at the back of the purse. I poked my husband. "Look," I whispered. "The tickets for Harold and Louise. I forgot to put them in the mailbox!"

My attention suddenly turned from the minister to thoughts of our dear friends getting dressed for the evening, going out of their way to drive to our house for the tickets and then finding an empty mailbox.

I was restless for the remainder of our trip. I couldn't wait to get home and phone or write. I sent Louise a note of apology and enclosed a lace handkerchief as a peace offering.

THANK YOU, LORD, that Louise and I are still good friends. You provided the grace for us to have a good laugh over my senior moment.

Promises, Promises

Dear God:

My friend Bev was absent from our choir practice the night the director handed out practice cassette tapes. He wanted members to listen to the songs over the weekend as preparation for a major rehearsal prior to the church Christmas service.

I offered my tape to Bev to use while my husband and I were out of town for the weekend.

"We're leaving before dawn," I told Bev, "so I'll put the tape in an envelope with your name on it and leave it at your doorstep."

Bev was grateful for my offer of door-to-door service.

Several hours and hundreds of miles later, Charles and I pulled into a rest stop for a drink and bathroom break. I reached into my pocket for some change for the drink machine. My hand landed on the tape case! I was horrified. There was no turning back. To make things worse, I had left my phone and address book at home. I hadn't planned to call anyone while I was on vacation.

Fortunately my husband remembered that his address book was in the car. He had the number of another choir member, so I called our friend Susan and spilled out my tale of woe.

"Don't worry," Susan said calmly. "I'll call Bev and share my tape with her. I'll listen to it first and then pass it on. I'll even deliver it."

I knew I could count on Susan. She's only thirty-nine—too young for a senior moment!

BUT THE MOST comforting truth of all is that I can count on *you,* dear Lord.

Not a Day Over ...

Dear God:

Last night I picked up Ruth for choir practice. We talked about the day's events as we drove. We sat next to each other in the choir loft. I remember her saying she almost didn't make it to rehearsal.

"Why?" I had asked. "You *never* miss!"

She looked at me and frowned. "It's my *birthday,*" she declared. "Tom and the twins were going to take me out to dinner, but at the last minute we decided to wait till the weekend."

Her *birthday!* My stomach turned over. I felt so dumb. I'd forgotten. Ruth was hurt, of course. She's my best friend. I'm her best friend. I've celebrated over forty birthdays with her. She's never forgotten mine. We've exchanged special gifts, enjoyed beautiful dinners and never missed these opportunities to be together.

But there I sat—without a card or gift and without even a thought about *her* day till that moment.

"Happy birthday," I said, and reached for her hand. "I'm so sorry. I don't know what happened. Had one of those senior moments, I guess. Please forgive me."

Ruth grasped my hand, then leaned over and whispered into my ear. "I nearly forgot my own birthday," she said, "till

Don woke me up singing, 'Happy Birthday.'"

Fortunately for those of us who know *you*, Lord, we are never forgotten or overlooked and we are always forgiven. You say in your Word that you knew us before we were knit together in our mother's womb.

I PRAY THAT you will bless my friend with a special Holy Spirit hug and the assurance that even if her best friend on earth forgets her birthday, her *true* best friend never will.

Lights Out

Dear God:

I can't keep this one to myself. My friend Carmen wrote to tell me about her teenage daughter who had a senior moment. Connie had strung Christmas lights around her room this year for some festive holiday lighting. A few days after Christmas she took them down and packed them in a box to use the following year.

That night was especially cold and rainy, Carmen reported. "Suddenly the electricity went out, as it often did in that house," she said.

Carmen decided to go to the store to get some additional flashlights and batteries. "Before I left I ran into Connie outside her room as my other kids were coming up the stairs. I let everyone know what I was up to."

Connie spoke up. "If only I hadn't taken down my Christmas lights, we ..."

Carmen and the kids looked at her, suppressing their giggles. Then Connie seemed to realize what she had just said. Her face turned bright red but she didn't let on. She simply walked into her room calmly, head held high, and shut the door! "The other kids and I stood there and laughed so hard we cried," said Carmen.

I LOVE KNOWING that *you're* the only light that really matters, Lord—and you never turn off or go out. And you help us laugh at ourselves when we appear to "lose" it.

Memory Hook

Dear God:

My dad, bless his heart, loved to read. He liked watching politics on television. He enjoyed a good conversation with friends and family. So it really bothered him when his memory began to slip. He didn't want to sit on the sidelines. Nor did he want to work hard at pulling names and dates and events from a memory bank that simply didn't deliver the goods as it once had.

He decided to do something about it. He considered listening to a tape, but his hearing was failing so that was out. Enroll in a seminar? No, he'd probably fall asleep in the middle. How about a book? That was it. He could read as much or as little at a time as he wanted, and he could go back and review what he'd learned.

One weekend while visiting my sister in Riverside, California, he decided to stop by B. Dalton Books. He asked at the desk where to find a book that would help his ailing memory. The clerk suggested *The Memory Book,* a popular title at the time.

Dad said later that he looked it over, was impressed with the summary on the cover and decided to buy it. He brought it to the cashier, where he paid for it with cash on hand. Then he and my mother left the store, strolled through the mall, had lunch, rested on a bench and watched the passing scene. As they walked toward their car at the end of the day, my father suddenly realized he did not have the book with him! "I must have left it at the bookstore," he said to Mom.

They hurried back to B. Dalton and sure enough, there it was—on top of the counter where my father had laid it while returning his wallet to his back pocket.

Then he strode out of the store once again, clutching the book under one arm and shaking his head. "I certainly need this book," he quipped to my mother. "The challenge will be in remembering to read it!"

IF I FORGET anything important, I know you'll remind me, Lord, as you've promised to do.

Everything in Its Place

Dear God:

Thank heaven I never have trouble finding things—well, almost never. Come to think of it, I did misplace my favorite necklace three times—once by putting it in a place so well-protected that I was afraid to look there lest a safety device sound an alarm and send the police to my doorstep. Then I found it, promptly lost and found it again and finally put it in a drawer by my bed.

And I did bury that gift check from Aunt Jen under a pile on my desk, so I wouldn't misplace it! Finally found it when I was forced to go through the paper trail at Aunt Jen's prompting, so she could balance her bank statement.

But one woman I heard about has me beat by a long shot. "When I lose something," she reported, "the first place I look is in the refrigerator."

How odd, I thought at the time. I'm glad I'm not *that* strange. Well, that was a couple of years ago. Recently, I decided to use my curling iron on my newly cut hair. I generally keep the iron in the vanity drawer in the bathroom. But I hadn't been in that drawer for some time, so when I opened it I was surprised the curling iron was not in its usual place. I couldn't imagine where else it could be. Clearly it was something I only used in the bathroom.

Annoyed, I walked into the kitchen to pour a glass of iced tea. Perhaps a few minutes of quiet, I thought, would bring a solution to the mystery. I didn't have long to wait. I opened the refrigerator, and as I reached for the pitcher, I noticed a shiny rod attached to a long black wire jammed between the carton of eggs and a bowl of tuna salad at the back of the top shelf.

My curling iron! *"No!"* I thought. "Why, I'm just like that lady I heard about." Then I burst out laughing as I remembered what happened. I had curled my hair in the kitchen the day my sister was visiting so she could use the bathroom. Then I got busy fixing lunch. Apparently I had my hands full with the curling iron in one and a loaf of bread in the other. So I set down the iron on the top shelf and shut the door. Never noticed it again—until this day!

Mum's the word on that one, Lord. Please don't breathe it to a soul—even after we're all together in heaven.

I'M REMEMBERING that you said in your Word that my sins are as far from you as east is from west. I hope that applies to senior moments, too!

Why Didn't I Think of That?

Dear God:

My kids are still in their thirties, though one is about to topple into her forties. Can it be? It seems I just turned forty myself. And then suddenly (twenty-two years later) here I am holding my Golden Age Passport, good for free admission to any national park in the United States. And I'm over the age hump when it comes to movies. I get the senior discount every time. And I now qualify for 10 percent off at Rubio's Restaurants. Makes me wonder if what happened to my friend will happen to me before I know it!

She and her daughter went out for burgers one day and as they stood in line to order their food, my friend said to her daughter, "Let me order for us because I have a senior citizen card."

Her daughter looked at her mom with a quizzical expression, as if to say, "Mom, have you forgotten how old I am?"

Instead she simply waved *her* senior citizen card in the air and said with a smile, "I have mine, too, Mom. This lunch is on *me!*"

Then on the way home my friend stopped to fill up her car with gas. As she was about to replace the cap to the gas tank, she dropped it and it rolled under her car. She knelt down and reached for it, but it was too far from her grasp. With a sigh, she entered the station and asked if anyone had a stick or a pole she could use to retrieve the cap. A man standing in line, waiting to pay, smiled, cleared his throat and then said politely, "Ma'am, may I suggest you drive the car forward a bit and then you'll be able to pick up the cap?"

OH, LORD, it's tough to be reminded of our weaknesses. Help me to receive advice when I need it.

A Day of Rest

Dear God:

You know how to turn a senior moment around, and I'm certainly glad you did so for my husband. After forty-four years of marriage and farming together in the heat and cold of central Kansas, I guess it's natural for a little mix-up to occur from time to time.

You know that wheat harvest is the busiest time of the year for us, with over half our year's earnings coming in at that time. I've always been happy (and maybe a little proud!) that unlike many of our farming friends, we do *not* cut wheat on Sunday.

We've always dedicated that day to you, Lord, as a time of worship and much-needed rest. Funny how that changed one day in the middle of harvest season.

I noticed my husband was awake and up early on a Sunday morning. I was surprised because I knew how tired he had been and how much he had looked forward to a good long sleep and a bit of pampering.

"Aren't you going to stay in bed for your Sunday foot massage?" I asked, playfully.

"Is this Sunday?" I could tell he was surprised by my question. "I was ready to head for the field," he said. He looked a bit flustered—but also relieved. At seventy-two some of these "moments" are occurring more frequently.

"Now I've got to call the hired man and tell him I made a mistake. When I told him to meet me at the field this morning, I thought it was Saturday," he said. My husband made the phone call, smiled at me, then pulled off his shoes and socks and plopped his feet in my lap!

YOU KNEW, dear God, that he needed a day of rest, time in the Word and fellowship with other believers—but first that foot massage!

Locked Out

Dear God:

I can't order off the senior menu at Coco's. I don't qualify for senior admission to the movies, and I'm just barely old enough to join AARP! Yet I'm *behaving* like a senior. I'm having those "moments" they all talk about. Just call me Forgetful, especially without my husband to remind me of what to do. I can't wait for him to come home. Guy's month long visit with his mother has left me feeling lonesome and lonely at the same time. Did you see what I did yesterday afternoon? I was loaded down with a ton of groceries and mail and odds and ends. Getting the key in the door lock was quite a feat! Getting it out must have seemed like a monumental task—because the next morning I noticed I hadn't done it. There, dangling from the lock, were my keys. They had been hanging there all night. Talk about an invitation to a thief—it couldn't have been more clear!

Thank you for taking care of it for me. I can just picture a huge angel watching over my apartment while I slept peacefully, totally unaware of what I had done—or not done.

You hold the keys to the Kingdom. *You* open doors no one can shut, and *you* shut doors no one can open (Is 22:22).

That night, you weren't opening. You were keeping watch over me. Thank you for taking care of me—especially when I seem unable to take care of myself.

WHAT A COMFORT it is to know you never slumber nor sleep!

Poignant Moments

Wait for the Lord; be strong and take heart and wait for the Lord.

PSALM 27:14

Marbles, Anyone?

Dear God:

Mother and the rest of our family have always enjoyed playing games. So when Mom, now eighty-three years of age, planned to come south from Amarillo, Texas, to Odessa in February to visit me for a week, I began to think of some fun games we could play together.

Mother lives alone and still drives—at least to Wal-Mart and to church. She's also in pretty good health. But shortly after she arrived, I noticed that her short-term memory had begun to decline. It seemed to coincide with a recent diagnosis of arteriosclerosis.

The third evening she was in our home, my family and I decided that a good game of Scrabble would be a fun way to pass the time. It's quiet, slow-moving and doesn't require any physical energy. After reviewing the rules of the game and setting out a hot ginger drink, Mother and I began building our words.

She's always been known for her ability to spell almost any word, so when I noticed her struggling with spelling, I became concerned. And the longer we played the more confused she became about some of the positions of the words on the game board.

More than halfway through she grew tired of thinking. She

turned to me with a quizzical expression. I could see the fatigue in her gentle eyes.

"Can't we just play marbles?" she asked.

I laughed, then she laughed. We folded up the board and put it away.

As I lay in bed that night I became aware that Mother's life, like our game of Scrabble, would one day fold up—much sooner than I was ready for. A tear trickled down my cheek.

I wondered where I might buy some marbles!

AND I ALSO promised myself that I would spend more special moments with my mother. Thank you for the gift of her in my life.

Bossy

Dear God:

Today I'm thinking about my dad and my uncle. Hard to believe they're gone. I remember them passing away in 1997, just a few weeks apart. I like knowing they're together with you. Then two years later Mom died and left only one sibling—her younger sister. The family is getting smaller.

I'm so glad I attended the reunion recently with Dad's children and the surviving brothers and sisters. It was fun to hear our cousins talking about past and future reunions. With dad's two sisters ages eighty-one and ninety-one, I knew they wouldn't be around for many more reunions. I had to laugh when one cousin asked, "Well, what do you have planned, Marion? You were the boss when we were kids, always telling us what to do. So, what *are* we going to do?"

He was right—and everyone agreed. I had been bossy! I liked deciding what game we'd play and how to play it.

After the reunion, I began thinking about what he had said. Suddenly the reason he said it became clear. Since I'm the firstborn grandchild on both sides of our family, why, I'll be the matriarch when my aunts are no longer around. What a sobering thought! I'm already part of the "older generation."

I can see that many of the elders are looking to me for stories of the history of our family. So, what *am* I doing about it,

Lord? Learning all I can about our parents and grandparents in a genealogy library, visiting the birthplace and childhood homes of our paternal grandparents and tracing the history back to the 1700s.

God, I want to leave a legacy for our children, grand-children and great-grandchildren that will give them pride in their heritage and a sense of what it took for their ancestors to become the doctors, accountants, ministers, teachers and writers they were. And as I learn more about their great faith in you, Oh Lord, I am reminded of the old hymn that bids us to set an example for future generations—so that all who come behind us will find us faithful.

I LIKE TALKING to you about this, Lord. I see that my responsibility as the "oldest" is to make sure that faith is passed on and our descendents will learn of our trust in and love for you. If I can succeed in doing that, then all the moments of my life will have been worth living.

Eyes to See, Ears to Hear

Dear God:

I remember a particular night in February 1995 when my mother spent the night with me. She had difficulty sleeping. She talked incessantly. I reminded her over and over to go to sleep, but she ignored me and just rattled on.

Then something she said really touched me. "You know, you think you're ready to meet the Lord, but when the time comes, you're not sure you're ready to step over that line."

I realized then her time on earth might be coming to a close and she sensed it. I lay down, and this time I listened intently to what she was saying. Hours passed. Then suddenly she sat straight up in bed. "Look! Look at that light!" she exclaimed.

"Mom, it's the middle of the night!" I said, a bit annoyed.

"But I've never seen light like that before," she continued.

At that point I realized she truly was seeing something. I nearly leaped across the bed and sat beside her. Her blind eyes were riveted on the scene she was describing. "Look at those beautiful green hills. I've never before seen the color green like that."

I watched intently as her eyes moved from side to side. Lord, it seemed you were giving her a preview of heaven. It wouldn't have surprised me if you had whisked her away before my very eyes. I remember how she continued to describe the lovely scene that only she had eyes for. And then she gasped.

"Why, there are some of my cousins!" she said with excitement in her voice. "They've been dead for years."

She called out their names as if taking roll call as they appeared to her. I waited breathlessly to see if you would give her a glimpse of my dad, my two brothers and my sister. But you did not. It might have been too painful for Mother to see them at a distance and not be able to touch them.

About an hour later Mother lay back on her pillow. She laughed and then cried out, "Oh, you precious little babies! Come to Grandma." Stretching her hands upward she began making a tickling motion. Her arms moved from one "baby" to another as her eyes focused on the images she was seeing. "They must be little cherubs," I thought. She'd always loved babies and couldn't wait to get her hands on them.

By then I was almost certain that would be her last night on earth, and I was filled with a mixture of sadness and happiness. God, I recall telling you my feelings that night. I would miss her so much. She was sad, too—about leaving me—but happy that she'd be in heaven with you and the rest of our family.

But you had other plans for Mom. She lived on for five more months before you called her home.

THANK YOU, LORD, for that heavenly encounter that helped Mother, when the time came, to step over the line to meet you. A rare moment. A poignant moment. One to celebrate.

On the Move

Dear God:

I have too many *things*. How will I ever decide what to keep and what to discard, if I have to move?

I've been thinking about this for some time, as I watch friends and relatives relocate to retirement homes where there is little space for personal belongings. I have a huge collection of gospel music tapes that mean a lot to me. My daughter Pam said she has a large basement, and I could store them there. But she lives in Virginia, and I live in Pennsylvania, so they wouldn't be available whenever I wanted them.

Last summer at our annual cousins' reunion, I talked about this dilemma with some of the other women. One of the ladies, who had recently moved into a small cottage at a retirement home, shared her perspective.

"I found that one's health plays an important part in deciding what to keep and what to part with when you're ready to move," she said. "One gets to the point in life where 'things' no longer matter as they once did."

I appreciated her point of view.

It seems you provide whatever we need whenever we need it, dear God. You not only put desires in our heart, you take them away at the right time, as well. Thank you. I'm not going to lose another moment's sleep over a decision that I'm not yet ready to make.

WHEN THE TIME COMES, I'll know what to do because you'll guide me every step of the way.

Telling It Like It Is

Dear God:

As they say, "Out of the mouths of babes"—which I know first-hand from teaching children's worship to the two- to five-year-olds. This year Valentine's Day fell on a Sunday, as you know. I decided to make our Sunday school class really special that day with a valentine for each of the kids, candy hearts and strawberry punch.

I used some new makeup that even my teenage daughter approved of! Then I put on my red suit, which I hadn't worn in months. I felt quite spiffy—and attractive—for a grandma!

Later that morning as I helped a four-year-old glue a valentine together, I bent over his shoulder to show him what to do. He looked up at me with a furrowed brow and questioning eyes.

"Gee, you must be old," he remarked. "You got lots of wrinkles!"

I can only imagine the look on my face, as I glanced up at my husband, who was my helper that day. "Doesn't that just make your day?" he teased.

Then, Lord, I remembered your reminder in Proverbs 16:18. "Pride goes before destruction, a haughty spirit before a fall."

I passed out valentine cookies to the children. And for me? I thought about eating crow!

I felt 100 percent better when two of my friends shared similar experiences with me. Yvonne said that while teaching her Sunday school class she noticed a little girl watching her closely as Yvonne told a Bible story. "I was so inspired by the child's rapt attention," she said, "that I became even more animated as I relayed the details."

Finally, the little girl was unable to hold herself back another minute. She waved her hand at Yvonne, who was certain the child had just gained a compelling insight that she was eager to share with the rest of the class.

"I thought I had really reached them that day," Yvonne later told me with a touch of pride.

"You know what?" the child had asked, sounding as if she were on the verge of an important announcement.

Still watching Yvonne's face intently, she said boldly, "Your skin sure is getting old!"

"So much for biblical insights and for a lesson in pride," said Yvonne, laughing.

I could relate to this experience from my own life. While baby-sitting three of my grandchildren, my four-year-old granddaughter looked at me across the breakfast table one morning and asked, "What are those long things on your face?"

I gulped, then looked right into her eyes and said with a lilt in my voice, "They're wisdom wrinkles. Someday you'll get them, too. They're what God gives older people who trust in him."

THANK YOU, LORD, that I (and other wrinkle-faced friends) can put all our hope and trust in *you!*

Sunday Escape

Dear God:

According to Rose, she and Frank, who met and married while living in a retirement/nursing home facility, enjoyed their new life together as husband and wife. They especially delighted in long drives in the country and eating dinner out on Sundays after church.

One Sunday as Frank drove his sedan down the driveway with Rose at his side, he noticed two elderly women walking together along the sidewalk leading out of the complex. He stopped and rolled down the window. "Would you like to go to church with us?" he asked.

"Oh, yes," one answered quickly. The other smiled and nodded in agreement.

Following the morning service, Frank extended another invitation. "How about joining us for lunch at Elbie's?" he asked.

"Not Elbie's," said one. "We were just there last week."

No problem. Frank was happy to oblige. It was a beautiful day, perfect for a drive. He mentioned a restaurant about fifty miles away, and everyone agreed it was a fine idea.

"What nice women," Rose whispered to Frank as the women walked ahead of them into the restaurant. "They're so easy to be with."

"We'll have to spend more time with them," said Frank.

Later that day, after a good meal and a pleasant return drive, Frank pulled the black sedan into the driveway of the senior complex. "Which unit is yours?" Rose asked the ladies.

One of them answered for both. "We don't know," she said, smiling.

Before Rose and Frank could decide what to do next, they noticed two police cars parked nearby.

Frank turned off the motor and helped the women out of the backseat.

Two nurses stepped forward with the policemen not far behind.

"Thank heaven," said one. "You're safe. Where have you been?" she asked.

The ladies weren't at all certain, but they assured the nurses they had had a wonderful time! Rose and Frank soon learned that the women had "escaped" the facility through the alarm-set doors.

Everyone breathed a sigh of relief as the policemen hopped into their patrol cars and backed down the drive. It all ended well. But Frank and Rose decided that in the future, before inviting any sweet elderly people to join them for church and lunch, they would ask a few important questions!

Everyone can use a break. But "breaking out"—well, that's another matter!

WHAT WE *REALLY* need, Lord, is to *break free*—by turning to you for our every need and desire.

Making Music—With What's Left

Dear God:

There are those moments that make us laugh—thank you that we can laugh. Sometimes it's all we can do when we feel old and foolish. But there are also those moments that are so poignant they take our breath away. I remember reading about such a time in an article about Itzhak Perlman, the violinist, published in the *Houston Chronicle*.

People who attended his concerts regularly knew what to expect whenever he came onstage. Perlman had been stricken with polio as a child and had to walk with a brace on each leg and steady himself with crutches.

"To see him walk across the stage one step at a time ... is an unforgettable sight," Jack Reimer reported in his article. "He walks painfully, yet majestically, until he reaches his chair. Then he sits down slowly, puts his crutches on the floor, undoes the clasps on his legs, tucks one foot back and extends the other foot forward. Then he bends down and picks up the violin, puts it under his chin, nods to the conductor and proceeds to play."

The audience is used to this ritual, and they sit patiently, knowing it will be worth the wait. But one evening something unexpected happened. He had just begun to play when suddenly one of his strings snapped. The sound was unmistakable! Everyone in the room must have been aching for him. What could it mean—putting on the braces again, picking up the crutches and limping offstage to get another violin or to find a string to repair the one he had?

But no, none of the above occurred. In fact, Perlman himself surprised the audience with his next move. He signaled the conductor to start again. The orchestra began, and Itzhak Perlman, master violinist, *played from where he left off.*

Everyone who knows anything about violin playing knows it's impossible to play a symphonic work with only three strings. "But that night Itzhak Perlman refused to know that.... He played with such passion and such power and such purity as they [the audience] had never heard before," the paper reported.

He drew out *new sounds*—perhaps new even to him! And when he finished, the audience sat in wonder and stillness— but only for a moment. Then they rose to their feet in a sudden burst of appreciation, cheering and clapping, screaming and applauding.

And how did the master musician respond? He smiled, wiped the perspiration from his forehead and raised his bow to quiet the room. "Sometimes," he said, "it is the artist's task to find out how much music you can still make with what you have left."

DEAR LORD, what a lesson there is here for me. Help me to make my music today with everything I've got, and when the time comes to slow down, show me how to make it with what I have left.

Jesus Loves All His Children

Dear God,

"Jesus loves the little children!" How easy it is to belt out the title of that favorite song—especially when singing it with my three-year-old granddaughter, Mairin. I have only to look at her and her sister to know that you do love the little children of the world. And I know you love the big ones, too. I'm trusting that you love the older kids, as well. We sure need your love, O Lord. I know I do.

You tell us in Scripture that to enter into the kingdom of heaven we must become as little children. Hard to imagine from the vantage point of twenty or thirty years! But now that I'm much older than that I see how some of us—including my own parents—have been swept into a second childhood by the mere fact of age. Bodies lose their youthful stamina and strength. Minds are not as sharp, emotions more fragile, thoughts simpler and less analytical. Mom is like a little child now—delighting in an ice cream cone, playing catch with a big beach ball, taking an afternoon nap.

Maybe the "second childhood" of old age isn't as bad as some make it sound. Why am I afraid of it—especially when you have called us to be as little children? Simplicity, innocence, dependence can be good things when practiced for the right reasons. When I surrender my "grown-up" ways you have more freedom to direct my path and to take over the burdens I strapped to my back the day I turned "adult." Maybe I need a perspective adjustment. Instead of fearing the loss of independence and hoping I'll never have to face it, let me be reminded as the days go on that you truly love the little, the big, the old, the young, the firm and the infirm *children* of the world—regardless of their ages or situations.

YOU ARE our God and we are your sons and daughters.

Good-Bye, Dear Friend

Dear God,

I'm feeling sad today. Another friend has died. The prognosis was good for such a long time. I can hardly believe Nancy is gone. People can die at any age, of course, but it's especially painful to wait and watch as someone I know well declines and dies. I'm even angry. That surprises me. I'm sure she didn't die on purpose—to hurt me, to get me all fired up. But still I miss her terribly. I didn't want our friendship to end this way. Things won't be the same without her. How can I ever play tennis again—without Nancy as my partner?

I remember when we first met. Fifth grade. She was the new girl in class, and our teacher, Mrs. Monroe, asked me to be her friend and welcome her into one of the games during recess. We played Crack the Whip that day, and I fell and cut my head and had to be rushed to the emergency ward at the hospital.

Nancy called me that night. She said she was worried about me. That day was the beginning of our long friendship. Fifty-five years long. God, I miss her so much. I'm aching inside. It helps me to know that you know what I'm feeling.

Of course, I like knowing Nancy is with you, Lord, free of cancer, dancing at your feet and singing your praises. Your timing is always perfect, I know that. But from a purely selfish point of view, I wish you had left her here a little longer.

Sometimes I close my eyes and there I am—with you and Nancy and my parents and so many others I haven't seen in so long. But it's not my time yet. I can tell. I still have a passion for life. And you've given me a mission here on earth. I'm not finished yet. Thank you for giving me more than one friend. Let me make the most of these relationships while I still have them. Friends are such an important part of our life, dear God.

HOW KIND OF YOU to give us these companions for our journey—people we can talk to, pray with, listen to, comfort and encourage. Like a patchwork quilt, they provide warmth and comfort but never smother.

Dog Days

Dear God:

I'm glad I remembered *your* name. I forget so many these days. For people in their seventies—like me—life is sometimes like the dog days of summer. Many former activities have slowed down or been eliminated. Health declines and spirits droop like garden flowers in the summer heat.

We've downsized from a large home to a small one. We've given up many treasures to save space. Sometimes we almost get cabin fever because we can't get out and go the way we used to. We've moved near our family so they can check on us. Or are they more interested in raiding our refrigerator and pantry? I've had to set some limits!

But we still count our blessings: We have an air-conditioned home, plenty of good food to eat, a comfortable bed (or a recliner chair) to sleep in. And most important, we have you, we have each other, and we have our memories. How you've blessed us through the years.

Actually, our dog days are short compared to the Israelites' forty years of wandering in the heat of the desert. And we can still see—so we can read your promises in the Bible rather than waiting for Moses to announce them.

You've said you'll never leave your children (no matter how old they are) nor forsake them, and you've assured us that you are preparing a place for us. Each day is one step nearer to our last moving day—the transition from earth to heaven. No longer will we have to pack and unpack and wonder, "Where did I put that?" We'll be caught up with you and the rooms in your mansion that you've set aside for us.

WHAT A MOMENT that will be!

Night-Light

Dear God:

Living alone is scary at times. I've told you about this before. Sometimes I wish there was somebody beside me—you know, somebody with *skin!*

I feel most alone at night. I suppose a little night-light would help to push away the darkness when I wake up. But this morning I'm glad I don't have one. Last night was a perfect example of how you take care of me. Remember how I fell into that restless sleep? I hate when I toss and turn wondering and worrying—mostly about silly things that I know you'll handle.

Anyway, dear God, I don't recall just when I awakened, but I do know the house was still—and bright—even without any lights on. I walked into the living room, then the kitchen, thinking I'd forgotten to turn off the porch light. I opened the door. No, I hadn't forgotten. My light was off. But *yours* was on—spilling across the lawn, the porch, the entire house.

How long did I stand in the doorway? I have no idea, so caught up was I by the beauty of the moonglow. I knew I wasn't alone. I knew I never would be—ever. For you are the light of the world, and you promise to be with us forever.

I pulled my robe closer around me as the cool night air caressed my skin.

THANK YOU, Oh God, for the eternal gift of your light.

From Gray to White—Overnight!

Dear God:

Did you hear what that woman said to me today at the conference? Well, of course you did! But can I tell you anyway—even though you already know. I love talking things over with you. You have a way of making me feel so special. I'm not even embarrassed to brag a little in front of you.

"You deserve the award for having the prettiest hairstyle of everyone here," the woman said as we passed each other on the walkway after lunch. "The other ladies in my cabin agree," she added. "And we all like your natural color."

I was stunned. That comment made my day, Lord. Imagine—*my* hair winning an award—even if it's only an imaginary one.

I have to laugh just thinking about it. Remember the day I discovered my first gray hairs? That must have been twenty or more years ago. I changed my hairstyle immediately to cover them up. Now I'm almost white and I'm getting rave reviews. The last two decades have gone by so fast it seems I've turned from gray to white overnight. So many things have changed—the divorce, new marriage, moving a hundred miles from the house I thought I'd live in forever, saying farewell to my dear father as he lay dying, helping my sister relocate our mother, starting a new facet of my career, becoming a mother-in-law and a grandparent. So much in so little time.

And here I am—today—living the golden years I read about in books long ago. Days that include walking in the park with my husband, collecting seashells with my granddaughters, watching an old movie with my son in his bachelor pad, working on a new book, climbing the rocks in the desert with my grandson, speaking at women's retreats, talking quietly with you as I am right now. Thank you for loving me, O Lord of my salvation, for holding me close during the scary times and cheering me on when I'm ready to fly. Changes, new choices and decisions are all part of the process of growing—and of growing older.

I KNOW THAT everything will fall into place at the right time and in the right way—as long as you're beside me.

Seeing With Hands and Heart

Dear God:

Mother had a different kind of senior moment—the kind that comes to many of us during our last years of life. It was hard to tell she was blind because she never complained. She simply learned to see with her hands and heart. She loved tending your vegetables, Lord! I admired her for keeping up with her gardening even after her sight began to fail. My brother-in-law planted whatever she wanted—tomatoes, beans and corn. She told him just where to place them so when they sprang up she could still do her own weeding—by feeling the difference between the vegetables and the intruders.

When we visited we were careful not to move anything without telling her. She had lived in that house for so long that she knew the *exact* location of every item and piece of furniture. How gracious you were to give her the ability to cook and wash dishes even without being able to see well. Sometimes she missed a few spots. If she got to talking she'd forget to run her hands over the plates to be sure they were clean.

On most Sundays after church a large crowd of friends and family gathered at her house to eat and visit. I remember one Sunday when Mama was washing dishes and talking happily while some of us dried and others put the dishes away. Whenever we found a plate she hadn't gotten quite clean, we'd slip it back in the dirty stack.

But she knew what was going on. "You girls don't have to worry about hurting my feelings," she'd say. "I know I've already washed this platter. I must have missed a spot."

The most remarkable thing about her was the way she used humor to see the things within. I remember when my husband and I were stationed in the military on an island off the coast of Alaska for three years. We hadn't seen Mama for all that time. When we finally visited her, we were all so excited everyone started laughing and hugging and talking at the same time.

"Honey," Mama said to me, "you're just as pretty as ever."

My oldest sister intercepted the compliment. "Don't let it go to your head," she said with a playful smile. "That comment came from a blind woman."

Mama laughed. "There's more than one way to see," she added. "I always told you girls, 'Pretty is as pretty does.'"

I MISS MAMA, dear God. Although her eyesight failed here on earth, her ability to laugh and love never failed. I'm glad she's with you now, *seeing* everything there is to see in heaven.

Laugh Lines

Dear God:

You know me better than anyone. I've never been one to worry about growing old. Doing it gracefully was my aim. I exercised to keep as physically fit as possible and thought of my wrinkles as laugh lines (while slathering on lots of moisturizers). I decided never to dye my hair, preferring the natural gray as part of the beauty of old age.

In my late fifties, as a mother of four and grandmother of ten, I felt I had fulfilled my goal. I remained active as a writer, speaker, piano player, piano teacher and painter. I was in pretty good physical condition and optimistic about the future. I did not fear growing old.

Until a catastrophe changed my outlook. My aging mother suffered a stroke. Once an active craftsperson who whistled cheerfully through her days, she became depressed and inactive, even slovenly about her appearance and her house. My father suffered two strokes and a heart attack, resulting in increasing dementia. He forgot how to garden and eventually forgot that I was his daughter.

Dad wandered away from home on October 8, 2000.

Mom died on February 24, 2001.

Dad's body was discovered on April 19 the same year.

I suddenly felt old. No matter my outlook, no matter my

attempt to remain youthful, I was not in charge. And that was that!

Then one night after Dad's funeral, I dreamed Mom and Dad were talking together. Their bodies appeared young. Mom's beautiful brown eyes crinkled as she laughed. And Dad's smile lit up his cornflower-blue eyes.

Why fear old age? I asked myself when I awoke. It's not permanent. It's simply part of the necessary transition to eternal life with God. I'm active again, writing, playing piano, teaching, speaking. I exercise each day, keep putting on the face creams and still don't dye my gray hair, but I keep it neat and shining.

When a woman told me the other day, "No! You can't be sixty!" I replied, "Sure, I am!" Then a thought followed, "And going on eternal youth." I don't know what my earthly future holds. I may have inherited my parents' propensity to stroke. I may develop dementia, or life's trials may bring on depression. But I do know what my eternal future holds, and I rest in knowing it with certainty.

Lord, do you allow computers and pianos in heaven? Will you need artists and teachers? Just in case, I'm practicing every day. My body will eventually fade, but in mind and spirit I'm ageless.

ONE DAY, *you* will give me a new temple, a youthful body that will never grow old. When I feel frail, I look forward to that time, but just for today I'm thankful for the gift of what I have right now. I'm maintaining it to the best of my ability and living each day to the limit. Was that me I heard whistling?

Short Takes

They rejoice in your name all day long.

PSALM 89:16

Moment by Moment

Dear God:

Remember that song by the Beatles, "I Wanna Hold Your Hand"? That's me today. I wanna hold *your* hand, Lord! I need your wisdom and grace, and by the way, could you please focus my thoughts?

I returned home from the store today, and when I saw that the driveway was empty, I panicked. "Where's my car?" I shouted. I was *certain* it had been stolen. I can still feel the beat of my heart when I feared the worst. Then I paused to collect my thoughts—and finally breathed a giant sigh of relief when I realized I was *in* it!

I relaxed, however, when I heard that my neighbor spent twenty or thirty minutes one day wondering where she left her favorite pencil—only to find that she (a right-hander) was carrying it in her left hand!

THESE SENIOR MOMENTS are multiplying. Help, Lord!

Late Learner

Dear God:

I don't feel much different than I did when I was sixteen years old. I know a bit more, and I've had a world of experiences—some I'll never forget and some I'd rather forget, if you know what I mean.

I wish the sixteen-year-olds of today wouldn't treat me as though I'm *different*. I'm still the same *me* inside that I've been all my life. For that matter, even some twenty-, thirty-, forty- and fifty-year-olds don't get it. I'll be gone before they understand—just as those I didn't understand died before I finally got it. Now I know why my mother cried before she died. She said she finally understood her mother. Today *I* cry. I'm beginning to understand her. Will my children do the same over me?

"YOU, O LORD, keep my lamp burning" (Ps 18:28).

Future Thinker

Dear God:

I remember the elation I felt almost eight years ago when my first granddaughter, Lauren, was born. I had just turned fifty. Since then, I have fussed over her, been amazed by her, taught her and kept her safe whenever her parents entrusted her to my care.

Last week she suddenly asked, "Grandma, how old will I be when you're eighty?"

"You'll be thirty," I said.

"Oh, good, Grandma! Then I'll be able to take care of you!"

Tears welled in my eyes, as I caught a tiny glimpse of my future—the winter of my life. Her words warmed me like the morning sun. Little did Lauren know what an extraordinary gift she had just offered.

HOW PRECIOUS, LORD, is your love that flows from the hearts of your children.

Cold Feet

Dear God:

I know you caught me snickering when my husband carried in a gallon of milk from the store and set it down on the mat by the door, then took off his shoes, picked them up and carried them to the refrigerator. But I couldn't help it! It was so funny!

Maybe I did go a little too far when I offered to cook his favorite *shoes* for dinner. The look on his face made me laugh even more.

But I sure got a payback when I looked in the bathroom mirror that night after showering—in time to catch myself from spreading toothpaste on my underarms. That probably made you smile, too.

TIME FOR ME to claim Psalm 71:1: "In you, O Lord, I have taken refuge; let me never be put to shame."

I'm Too Young for This

Dear God:

Here I am nearly a decade ahead of the AARP gang, yet I feel like one of them! I'm having some of those "moments" they like to talk and laugh about. What's going on here?

A preview? So *that's* it. Thanks a lot, God.

I'd better get my act together or I'm going to be out of a job—paid or otherwise. What about this latest episode with my high school students? I've known all year that Fridays are my days to mentor them. How embarrassing, then, when I forgot to visit my assigned student last week. She had no idea what had happened to me.

Enough of that. I can't have people whispering about my forgetfulness when I can't even blame it on my age. I know what I'll do. I'll make signs on that bright, neon-pink paper I have—DON'T FORGET TO MENTOR TONIGHT—and tape them all over the house on Thursday evenings. Now if I can just remember where I put that paper—and the black marking pen I bought, and what day of the week it is....

I GIVE UP, LORD. It's time for me to let your Holy Spirit take over—to guide me in all my ways.

Wet Set

Dear God:

This morning Pete and I woke up and our bed sheets were soaking wet. What next? I thought. It had been a week of facing one age-related problem after another. I felt certain we had both gone incontinent overnight!

What a relief to find that it was our water bed—not us—that had sprung a leak!

THANK YOU for reminding me that I can lie down unafraid, and my sleep will be *sweet* (Prv 3:24).

Help Is on the Way

Dear God:

My friend Amina e-mailed me the other day with a tidbit that made my week! I now know I'm no longer alone in my forgetfulness or carelessness. She had dialed her daughter Susanna's phone number, using the auto dial on her keypad—#1 for her daughter, #2 for her son, #3 for emergencies.

The connection did not go through. Amina wondered if something was wrong with Susanna's answering machine. She tried again. The person on the other end asked my friend for her name and what help she needed. She hung up in frustration.

She decided to hit auto dial one more time.

A few minutes later the city police arrived at her door—saying they were responding to three 911 calls from her telephone!

"Now the local authorities have my number, all right," she quipped.

This incident brought me a good chuckle. I think I'll call her right now and tell her.... On second thought, e-mail is safer!

BETTER YET, I'm going to suggest she call you. You're always available twenty-four hours a day.

Living in the Moment

Dear God:

Help! Recently I had another senior moment at a critical time—while speaking with a friend. All of a sudden I couldn't for the life of me remember what I was about to say. Then suddenly the right words were there! We both laughed. It seems my "moments" are now stretching out to days and weeks. Oh, well, maybe it's not so bad after all. People are forever telling me to "live in the moment." I appear to be doing just that!

LORD, I AM so grateful that you will provide the words I need when I need them. All I have to do is ask.

Mirror, Mirror, on My Wall

Dear God:

Who's that old woman in my mirror? She appears to be an imposter! I think of myself as a seventeen-year-old, but my reflection shows my true age. I know it's foolish to protest, but I don't like what I see. I don't like the way my eyelids droop and my cheeks sag. Is this it? It won't get any better?

" 'Fraid so," I can hear you say. "But don't worry. *I* am more interested in your heart—and in your soul. *That* beauty will never fade."

The only prescription to keep that beauty at its best is *time spent with you.*

REMIND ME, DEAR LORD, to be beautiful in words and actions. Let me radiate joy and gratitude, the beauty that never fades.

It's a Bird, It's a Plane, It's ...

Dear God:

My husband told me with great enthusiasm this morning about a slate-gray bird he had spotted in the yard the day before. From his description we concluded it must have been a catbird.

"There's a problem, though," he said with a perplexed expression on his face. "I didn't see any whiskers."

"My dear," I said, choking back the giggles, "cat*fish* have whiskers, not cat*birds!*"

"Oh, you're right," he said and slunk out of the room. If he'd had a tail, it would have been tucked between his legs!

LORD, I'M SO GLAD you are our refuge when we are caught in those embarrassing senior moments.

Mother of the Bride

Dear God:

It's one thing to forget your best friend's name—but quite another to go blank when you're looking at your very own mother. I was the center of attention at a bridal shower my friend held in my honor. I was the only one who knew everyone in attendance, so it was clear that I should make the introductions.

I stumbled around the circle attempting to put together the correct faces and names. As I reached the last woman, I knew I was home free. My mother sat there smiling, as I stopped in front of her chair. I pulled her to her feet, slipped my arm around her shoulders and spoke up so everyone could hear. "I'd like you all to meet ... This is.... She's my mother. I mean, Mom, uh ..."

Oy vay! Blank mind. Blank screen. Blank page. I couldn't pull her given name no matter how hard I tried.

"I'm June Henderson," said my mother, glaring at me as if I were ten years old.

"Mom, of course, I mean June, I mean, everyone—this is my mother, June Henderson, and I'm her daughter...."

I'm a lot older now, but the lesson I learned that day has stuck. From now on I'll let people introduce themselves—even my mother.

BUT I WILL NOT hesitate to introduce you to my friends, Oh Lord, who hold the name above all names.

Thankful Moments

Give thanks in all circumstances, for this is God's will for you in Christ Jesus.

1 THESSALONIANS 5:18

A Peak Experience!

Dear God:

"Help, Lord, I'm having a senior moment!" Remember the day I hiked to the top of Mount Whitney? If ever I called for help—that was the day. I felt every bit of my fifty-seven years as we set foot on the trail that would lead us to the 14,496-foot peak in the Eastern Sierra Mountains in California. But now as I think about it with you, it's just a memory. But what a memory it is. Four of us—each one over fifty—determined to get to the top together. "All for one, one for all," we shouted as we slung our backpacks over our shoulders and trudged on without looking back for even an instant. Rain and fog clouded the panoramic view, but we kept on going. We had a goal to achieve—and we weren't about to let a little weather get in our way.

Later that day the sun broke through, lacing the clouds with rings of golden light. But it wasn't hot enough to penetrate the thick crust of snow that buried the ninety-two switchbacks leading to the ridge just below the summit. So we slogged through it, straight up, one deep step at a time, steadying ourselves with ski poles and calming our nerves with laughter and conversation (and many a silent prayer). I can still feel the adrenaline coursing through my body as I inhaled and exhaled the cold fresh air. Onward and upward to the top!

What a great moment when we reached the very top and signed our names in the guest log. We had done what thousands before us had done—scaled the highest peak in the contiguous United States. But we also had done so much more. We toppled our fear of height and cold and rain—and *age!* Making it to the top was more than a physical victory. It was a spiritual epiphany at the same time.

You gave each of us the grit, the stamina, the willingness and the perseverance to do something outside the commonplace. Thank you for the opportunity to risk, to dare, to challenge ourselves and to share the triumph of meeting our goal. Today as I look at the T-shirt that says, "I climbed Mt. Whitney," the bill cap with the Whitney logo and photos that help me relive the experience, I'm in awe of what I am capable of when you're with me, urging me on and affirming my strength.

HELP ME, Oh Lord, to press on toward all the high goals you have set before me.

Musical Chairs

Dear God:

My husband Hector is worried that one of us will open the draft on our coal stove in the basement, go upstairs and forget about it—and burn down the house! To ensure that does not happen, he worked out a plan. When he opens the draft and goes upstairs, he sets a chair at the top of the stairwell. And conversely, when he opens the draft and sits down to watch TV in the basement, he slides the old high chair over to the foot of the stairs. The chairs are his reminders.

He also likes to light a candle while we're watching television in the evening. One night last week, he forgot to blow out the candle before he came up to bed. It burned all night and, thankfully, caused no harm. But the experience scared him. Now, whenever he lights a candle, he sets that old high chair at the foot of the stairs to remind him.

The trick is to remember which chair means what! But if we forget, I'm sure John will come up with yet another plan.

Our children laugh at our unique game of "musical chairs." But I tell them, "Don't laugh. Your time is coming."

LORD, IT'S SUCH FUN to joke and laugh with our family. I don't ever want to let my age or my infirmities keep me from seeing the light side of life.

Stop! Look! Listen!

Dear God:

Getting older is getting old—if you know what I mean! I've decided that at this point I have two options: go with it, or push against it. I'm going to go with it. I'm too tired to fight the inevitable. Instead, I've decided to make the most of it—and even try to enjoy it. Therefore, I have committed to the following:

1. I'll stop lying about my age and start bragging about it.
2. I'll stop being defensive when people kid me about being off my rocker. I'll get up and prove they're right!
3. I'll stop waiting in line. Fewer things than ever before are worth the wait.
4. I will not turn back my "odometer." I've traveled a long way, and some of the roads weren't paved.
5. I'll focus on how young I feel instead of how old I am.
6. I'll keep in mind that I can't be over the hill without first getting to the top.
7. I'll remember that one must wait until evening to see how splendid the day has been.
8. I'll remind myself that being young is beautiful, but being old is comfortable.

9. I'll realize that old age is the time when former class-mates are so gray and wrinkled and bald they don't recognize me.

10. I'm going to learn to laugh at trouble today or I may not have anything to laugh at when I'm even older.

THANK YOU for setting me free from the fear of aging and the bondage of other people's opinions and approval. Help me to shine the light of your love—no matter what challenges I may face.

Cooking Lesson

Dear God:

After our five children left home, I realized I was still preparing food for seven instead of for two. Habit, I guess. I'd cooked for a crowd for so many years, I couldn't seem to downsize.

Now, however, my friends see me as something of an expert at cutting recipes in half. I've had to practice, but I've got it down to a science at last.

In order to do so, I've needed to brush up on my fractions. Do you know how much to use if your recipe calls for one-third cup sugar? One-half of one-third equals one-sixth. How much is one-sixth of a cup? There are sixteen tablespoons to a cup, so one-sixth of sixteen equals two and two-thirds tablespoons!

I'm weary just thinking about it. I don't dare try to cut complicated recipes in half at night. I'm brain-dead by then. If I'm going to make my husband's favorite desserts, I must do so first thing in the morning or not at all.

I'm not sure why I'm telling you all this, Lord. You know all about it—though I don't see anything in the Bible about you cooking and I hear there is no cooking in heaven. Is that true?

I've even learned how to use half an egg. I may be the first with this. My neighbor is fascinated with my creativity. I told her to break it into a measuring cup, beat it and use half. The other half is perfect to include in an omelet or for a hot egg sandwich.

Another way to solve the problem of too much food is to buy a bunch of small containers. And they don't have to cost much. At a used-clothing store I found two bags filled with small empty diet margarine tubs. They're perfect for storing extras—like a serving of spaghetti or a bit of leftover tuna casserole.

Some of my friends think I go too far with this. Why put myself through a math lesson every time I cook? Well, it seems I need the mental challenge.

Like last Saturday, for example. I made a cheese pie to take to the church fellowship dinner that night. I had bought a mix, with a beautiful photo of the finished product on the front of the box. I beat the eggs and added milk and cream cheese. I tasted it, but something seemed amiss. It was too sour. I hadn't seen sugar on the list of ingredients, however, so I didn't want to add it without knowing how much.

Maybe it's just me, I thought. Perhaps it would taste fine to others. I poured the mixture into the crust. Then I carefully swirled the strawberry gel across the top and popped the pie into the oven.

Later, as I was cleaning up the kitchen I found a small paper pouch on the table. Uh-oh! I suddenly realized the ingredients in this pouch should have gone into the pie!

How could I have forgotten in such a short time? I quickly opened the oven and checked the pie, but it was too set to remove the filling and add these additional items. My beautiful pie was ruined.

At the church dinner, I shared this experience with other ladies at the table where I sat. They all understood. They'd had similar senior moments! So we laughed it off and chalked it up to growing older. And each of us had a second helping of the bakery pie I had picked up on my way to the event.

THANK YOU, LORD, that I can let go of the little things. It's about time, isn't it? Good friends and laughter are much more important than a perfectly baked pie.

A Grandma's Heart

Dear God:

I'm thinking of my grandson Darian this morning. I miss him—even though we just had a great visit. But somehow it's never long enough, especially since we live so far apart. A four-hour drive from his house in Maryland to ours in New Jersey makes it a challenge to visit as often as we'd like.

We're so excited when we're together, but this visit was really special, Lord. Thank you for making it possible. It was the first time he stayed a whole week all by himself. What a handsome seven-year-old he is, tall, lanky, blond-headed with beautiful big brown eyes that twinkle. The little imp inside him shines through those eyes!

This past week was one of the best weeks of my life. Of course, it was also one of the most exhausting. I'm definitely having a senior moment. Every part of my body aches even though I slept till eleven o'clock this morning.

Play cars are strewn here and there, and his sneakers are still on my back porch. I'd like to leave them there forever. It warms my heart just to look at them. My mind is spinning with memories. I loved seeing Darian sing along with the other children at church, and I felt proud when he raised his hand to answer the pastor's questions. He wasn't shy in the least!

There were Mickey Mouse pancakes three days in a row, scrambled eggs turned brown on the ends and plenty of little sausages that I lovingly prepared. Poor kid! He had to listen to my speech about how sausages have high fat content and should be eaten sparingly!

Not every part of the week was fun for Darian. He bit his tongue while jumping in the pool. And then a bee stung him! And me? Well, my poor brain is worn out from answering all the questions he asked during our visits to science museums and the planetarium and while reading books and articles. And what about that game of Monopoly that lasted three days?

My grandma heart broke a few times at bedtime when he cried, "I miss my mommy." But I knew what to do—thanks to you, Lord. I sang the same lullabies to Darian that I had sung to his mother when she was a little girl, the ones my mother sang to me and her mother had sung to her. What a blessing!

I know I'm an old-fashioned sentimentalist, and I know I'm bone-tired, but as I look at his pool toys in the garage and his sneakers by the door, tears of love and joy well up in my eyes and a lump forms in my throat.

I can only wish for many more senior moments like this, even if they're accompanied by hot flashes because I've been too busy to remember to eat my soy. My whole body aches because I haven't done the exercises I need to do to control the pain from arthritis! But I'm not complaining, God. I'll catch up on my self-care program in the days ahead. In the meantime, it's comforting to my soul to indulge myself in this moment of reminiscing.

THANK YOU, O, LORD, for blessing me with dear little Darian and for the week Grandpa and I enjoyed so much.

Lost and Found

Dear God:

How faithful you are! My friend Sarah told me about the time she had hoped to attend a writers' conference. Unfortunately, she didn't have the necessary funds when she needed them. Retired missionaries don't usually have extra cash stashed away for such opportunities, and she hadn't saved ahead for this event.

Still, Sarah felt led to go, so she filled out the registration form as an act of faith. "Then I rummaged through a desk I seldom use," she said, "looking for something I had misplaced. That seems to be a common experience now that I'm a senior. I groaned when I couldn't find what I wanted. Then suddenly something caught my attention. Nestled in the midst of a stack of paper was an uncashed check."

How did that get here? she wondered. Sarah pulled it out and stared in disbelief. The check was made out to her for one hundred dollars. Then it all came back in vivid detail. A friend from Canada had sent Sarah the check more than two years before. It was meant to go toward a visit to Brazil, where she was a missionary at the time.

"I vaguely remember telling my friend I couldn't find it," Sarah recalled. "But it didn't matter because the Lord had provided what I needed at the time. I forgot about the check and I assume my friend did, too."

But you did not forget, Oh Lord. It was as though you had placed it in reserve until the time Sarah needed it.

"I ran to the phone," Sarah told me, "and dialed Georgia's number—my friend in Canada. 'You won't believe what I found today,' I stammered. 'The check you sent me in 1999, for my Brazil trip! It just turned up. Wanted you to know I'll be using it toward the tuition for a writers' conference I'm eager to attend.'"

Sarah said her faith was reinforced that day. She knew then that you, dear God, would provide the necessary funds for the remainder of her tuition. "My senior moment literally paid off," she added with a smile.

THANK YOU, LORD, for providing for our every need—even the ones we don't know we have.

Garden-Variety Frustration

Dear God:

It looked so easy when I started. Okay, I'm no master gardener, but how hard can it be to plant a few trees? You move a little dirt around, dig some holes, and slip the trees out of their tubs into the waiting soil, add some water and fertilizer and voila! Before long I'd be picking fresh fruit from their limbs, reading a novel and sipping lemonade under their branches!

Okay, so I didn't think it through properly. I didn't know at the time that when I started digging I'd have to haul bucket-sized boulders out of one-foot-wide holes. No one told me what to expect. Lord, why didn't you drop a hint or two? I could have saved a lot of time and labor. Maybe you knew I needed the exercise. Thanks a lot!

Remember how frustrated I got? Sweat and struggle. That's the name of this game. I was about to burst into tears when I said, "'Nuf's enough." I couldn't take it anymore. I marched into the house, slammed the door good and hard, washed my face and hands, made a pot of tea, drank a cup, cried for ten minutes and asked you what to do.

I don't recall your answering me right away. I guess you thought it best that I have one of those "be-still-and-know-that-I-am-God" kind of moments. You're right. I needed one. I won't argue about that.

Later that day, there you were—speaking to me through my neighbor, who offered to get a backhoe to dig the holes. Notice I did not hesitate! I agreed on the spot, and within fifteen minutes all five holes were dug.

I can just see it now: leaves gently swaying in the wind, luscious peaches ripening on the vine and me—sitting under the branches reading a novel, sipping lemonade and praising your name!

HALLELUJAH!

Open-and-Shut Case

Dear God:

Talk about a senior moment! It turned into a two-hour nightmare. As I peer out of my glasses now, I'm reminded of how they might just as easily still be in Burlington, Ontario, Canada.

I walked out of Community Presbyterian Church one Sunday morning in April—the day before my appearance on the Canadian television program, 100 Huntley Street, fresh from the inspiring sermon and delighting in the brisk morning air. I felt free, excited and eager for what lay ahead.

I slipped off my clear glasses to exchange them for my sunglasses. Then I pulled on my warm jacket to shield me from the wind. I thrust my hands into the side pockets—checking, as my husband Charles has taught me to do, for each item I had brought with me. I had left my purse behind in the hotel room.

Kleenex tissues. Room key. Identification. Check! Check! Check! All there. Then panic set in. My glasses. Where were they? I had been wearing them just a moment before. I was certain I had returned them to my pocket. How could they have disappeared?

I couldn't lose them. Not now. Not in a foreign country. How would I get along? This is crazy-making. "What did you do?" I drilled myself.

I retraced my steps over the half-block from the church to where I was now standing. Back and forth I walked, looking at every square inch of pavement, in the street gutter, around bushes, under tall clumps of weeds. The glasses were nowhere to be seen.

Gone. Out of sight. Vanished.

I rushed back to the church and checked in and around the pew where I had sat. Then I dashed to the hotel to be sure I had really taken them with me. Maybe I hadn't been wearing them after all. By that point I didn't know what to believe. This was more than a mere senior moment. It was a disaster in the making. I had to have my glasses to see!

Then I became downright giddy. "Hang on, glasses. I know you're out there somewhere. I will not leave without you. You don't belong here. I mean, this is Canada and you live with me in the United States."

Oh Lord, I was sure I was losing it by then. I prayed like mad, remember? I returned once again to the route I had taken and looked at every speck of ground in front, behind and beside me. I *begged* you to show me the answer. People passing by probably thought I had gone over the top! I would have agreed with them.

Then I felt your counsel—to relax, breathe deeply, walk slowly, look up. And then it happened. I saw my glasses case with my glasses snuggled safely inside, sitting on top of a fire hydrant in front of an abandoned cottage.

"Hallelujah!" I shouted right there in the middle of the block on a Sunday morning in Burlington, Ontario, Canada— and I didn't care who heard me. I kissed the case and slipped it into my pocket, my right hand holding it firmly. Then I nearly skipped all the way back to the hotel.

But it was not until I stopped to thank and praise you that I really "got" the gift you had for me. "Look up, Karen. Up to me. And I will hear and answer you."

I'm still not sure how my glasses ended up on top of a fire hydrant. Perhaps a kind person found them on the sidewalk and placed them there for the owner to notice. Or perhaps even I laid them there for a second while I pulled on my coat and switched to my sunglasses. I simply don't remember the details. Nor do they matter.

HEAVENLY FATHER, what really matters is that this experience gave me an opportunity to do what you want me to do every moment of my life—senior moment or otherwise—and that is look up to you and depend on you.

Turn It Down, P-l-e-a-s-e!

Dear God:

Have I always been this sensitive to noise, to loud music, or is this just another "moment" that goes with being a senior?

"Turn it down, please," I shout to my grandkids as the CD blares.

Rock 'n' roll, soft rock, pop rock, Christian rock. It all sounds the same to me. *Loud!*

But there are those of us over sixty—like my husband Charles, for example—who would disagree. "Turn it up," he says, annoyed. "I can't hear it."

Apparently the young and the old have one thing in common—they like it *loud.*

I'm noticing that what I used to like I no longer care for, and what I once couldn't stand I now treasure—peace and quiet, time to think, to mull, to reflect, to be.

Shakespeare said, "To be or not to be, that is the question." For me it's not a question. It's a no-brainer.

To *be* is where it's at for me—at sixty-three!

Now *that's* music to *my* ears!

THANK YOU for the gift of sound and for the gift of quiet— and for the privilege of praising your name in every circumstance.

Big Spender

Dear God:

Good thing that some bill collectors have compassion. My husband told me he wrote a check to the phone company for the balance in his checkbook instead of for the amount on the statement. Now, there's a senior moment for you! If his social security check had been deposited before that stunt, Ma Bell would have received a nice chunk of change. On the other hand, if he had written the check for the phone bill after paying all the other bills, the phone company would have received $2.50. Thank you, Lord, that the person opening the envelopes spotted the discrepancy and alerted André to his error.

It is strange to observe ourselves behaving in such bizarre ways—doing things we wouldn't have done even a year or so ago. It's happening to me, too. So I can't point the finger at him alone.

A few weeks ago a client arrived at my home office for an appointment. He rang my unit number at the front gate. I answered and told him to press #9 on the keypad to let himself in. The moment I hung up I realized that I was supposed to press #9 on my phone keypad to let him in. Oh, no! I ran downstairs to meet him and there he stood, perplexed, punching #9 over and over to no avail.

My heart pounded. Should I admit my senior moment or dismiss it with a lie? "Well, we've been having a little trouble with that system. It's simply not reliable."

Then I was stopped cold in my spirit. I was the unreliable one. I couldn't even 'fess up to the truth. If I can't tell myself the truth, how can I expect to come clean with someone else?

It's all part of growing older, isn't it, Lord? We make mistakes. We forget. We don't do what we want to do. Then we're ashamed and embarrassed and we hide out, hoping no one else will notice.

BUT YOU'RE there, Lord. You know. You love me right through the senior moments. And you, like none other, have my true number. You even know the number of hairs on my head. (By the way, they're a little fewer this year than last year!)

Ups and Downs

Dear God:

When I step back and look at Charles and me as we get into bed at night, I have to laugh. It's a comedy of movement. One mattress cranks up. The other cranks down. One built-in massager soothes in waves, the other in soft rhythmic pounding. Here we are—two people who have slept together for nearly twenty years now sleeping on two separate mattresses with a common quilt. We need our space—at least for sleeping.

We used to look at ads on TV for new cars or vacation spots or the latest kitchen gadgets. Now a mattress that goes up and down like a seesaw captivates our attention. A good night's sleep is more important than a good meal at a great restaurant. Just another moment in the life of a senior.

We can't stay up till midnight, party past ten or fly the red-eye to the East Coast without paying the price. Those days are over. Now it's early to bed and early to rise—if we want to be wise!

I may miss out on a bit of late-night fun or a night-owl movie, but it's okay. I understand myself better these days. I know my limitations. And I'm beginning to see that recognizing what I can't do is as important as recognizing what I can do.

THANK YOU for showing me limitations as well as possibilities.

Balancing Act

Dear God:

What did you think of me on that video today? Do I really look that way when I walk? I felt as though I were trying to do a balancing act—one hand on my cane and the other on the handrail. I feel sad about it. I looked so old. Others were walking normally even though some are older than I.

What happened? I'd always been so active until two years ago when I had the back surgery for spinal stenosis. I hoped to be well by now. Why is the healing so long in coming? I don't mean to sound impatient, God, or ungrateful. At least I can look forward to a full recovery. Many people can't. I don't want to complain. You've provided many opportunities that I can participate in—water exercises that allow me to run, jump, walk, as well as swim. Thank you for blessing me so abundantly. My friends don't care how I walk or even how I appear when I walk. And I know you don't either, so why should I?

I feel better already—just being able to talk this over with you.

I LOVE YOU, LORD. No matter what my age or how infirm I may get, I'll always be your child.

The Whole Enchilada

Dear God:

I have to get this off my chest. I'm so glad you're willing to listen. I invited my daughter Jan to meet me for dinner at the Mexican restaurant in the Hundred Oaks Mall. But in my mind I was envisioning the Mexican restaurant at the Hickory Hollow Mall.

I remember that evening *too* well. I arrived about ten minutes early at the restaurant I had been *thinking* about. I called Jan on her cell phone to tell her I was inside waiting. She said she'd be there in five to ten minutes.

I wondered how she possibly could get there in such a short time. I predicted her drive to be about thirty minutes or more—but I didn't mention it. "She's an adult," I told myself. "I don't want her to think I'm questioning her judgment."

I walked into the restaurant and told the host I would wait for my daughter to join me before I ordered. People came and went and still no sign of Jan. I wasn't wearing my watch, but I knew more than ten minutes had passed. I munched on chips and dip till I was almost too full to eat. Then I ordered a soft drink.

A moment later I heard an announcement on the radio that was playing in the background. There had been a traffic jam about halfway between where Jan had been when we spoke and the restaurant where I was now waiting.

"Chill out," I scolded myself under my breath. "She's simply been detained in traffic."

More time passed, and by then I was feeling anxious—even worried. Was she in an accident? Did her car break down? I told the waiter I'd be back—just going to my car to make a call.

"Here," he said, pointing to a nearby courtesy phone. "Use this. It's for our customers."

I dialed Jan's cell-phone number.

When she heard my voice, she let out a huge sigh. "Oh, thank God you're alive and all right!" she exclaimed.

"Where are *you*?" I asked.

"Hundred Oaks, where we were supposed to meet," she replied. "Where are *you*?"

"Hickory Hollow, where I thought we were meeting," I said.

"I'll be right over," she said. "Don't move!"

She and a friend arrived within minutes and we dined together. Each of us shared our version of the misunderstanding. I discovered that night that my daughter *really* does care about me. She had called her brother—who lives with me—three times, and she phoned her older brother, as well.

She would have paged her dad but didn't have his beeper number. She also called the local hospital where I was a patient for triple bypass surgery the year before and for congestive heart failure six months afterwards.

"This girl *loves* her mother," her friend teased. "Jan was frantic and almost in tears when we couldn't locate you," she added.

Relief swept over us. Then we realized a lot of people were

waiting to hear the outcome. So Jan called her older brother first. "I found *your* mother!" she shouted. "*My* mama would never do anything like this."

She went on to tell him how Hundred Oaks seemed like a good place to meet, though I had been thinking of Hickory Hollow and went with that thought.

She and her friend then suggested that I purchase a small digital phone to carry with me. That way she and other family members would be able to reach me anywhere at any time.

I knew she was right—even though she's the daughter and I'm the mother! The next day I transferred my analog cell-phone account to a digital account and bought a small digital cell phone. But I still have a problem. I too often leave the house without it!

THERE ARE STILL times when no one but you, Lord, can reach me. When that happens, I know what I'll do. I'll rest easy and know that you are God—and you'll work out my dilemma.

Map of Time

Dear God:

Yesterday I took refuge in Proverbs 31:30—"Charm is deceptive, and beauty is fleeting; but a woman who fears the Lord is to be praised"—as I watched a "pretty young thing" at the supermarket and remembered looking like her many years ago.

Bob and I had just walked out of the store together. He checked the driveway in front of the store for passing cars before we crossed into the parking lot. The twenty-something woman with blond hair, flawless skin and legs to die for caught up to us and stood alongside my husband as he looked around a parked truck. I stepped up beside him on the other side and linked my arm in his.

"Is that your wife?" the woman asked, as though I were incapable of speaking up for myself.

My husband affirmed that I was indeed his wife. I added to his response. "Yes, I belong to him," I said and nestled in closer.

The woman looked me over from head to toe. "I like your hairstyle," she said. "It really suits you."

"Thank you," I replied, feeling more relaxed now that I realized she was looking at *me* and not my husband.

"You sure look good for your age!" she shouted as she crossed in front of us and headed for her car.

I was so disarmed I didn't know what to say.

What part of that sentence did she emphasize? *Look good* or *for your age?*

Still, I was flattered—sort of.

"I wonder just how *old* she thinks I am!" I said to Bob.

"Enjoy the compliment," he replied. "Don't analyze it."

I decided Bob was right. Maybe my beauty is fleeting, but at least someone still noticed what's left.

With head held high, I skipped across the driveway, pulling him along behind me. I may not look like twenty-something anymore, but in that moment I sure *felt* like it.

THANK YOU, LORD, that you are not preoccupied with our age—that no matter how old we get, we'll always be the apples of your eye.

The Big C

Dear God:

Can it be less than a year since "the big C" invaded our lives? So much has happened since then. I remember well the morning after we received the news that Charles had prostate cancer. I was to leave early that day for Indiana, where I was invited to speak at a mother-daughter banquet.

"Breakfast is ready," he had called from the kitchen as I put on the last touch of my makeup.

"Thanks. I'll be right there," I shouted from the bathroom.

Then I checked my list to make sure I had packed everything I needed for my flight.

I ran into the kitchen, gulped the protein drink he had prepared, ate the poached eggs hurriedly and poured a cup of tea into my thermos. I was all set.

"You're sure it's all right with you if I go?" I asked one last time.

"Absolutely," said Charles. "We've been over this before. I want you to keep living your life as you always have. I'll be fine, really."

"But it feels wrong somehow. My thoughts are as scattered as shells on the beach. I can't think straight."

I was having one senior moment after another. I had misplaced a book I wanted to take along, and my favorite bookmark was missing, too. I hate losing things. I ran from room to room looking through drawers, checking shelves, fingering pockets. Nowhere. I felt so frustrated. Then one last thought crossed my mind. "Check briefcase."

I did and there it was—the bookmark. Then a final inspection of a pile of printed material on my office sofa. *Voilà!* The missing book. "But I just looked there moments before," I said aloud.

What is happening to me? I wondered. Under normal circumstances I am an organized, orderly person. But these were not normal circumstances.

Just a week before, Charles had called me on my cell phone as I laughed and talked with two friends over lunch. "This time I do have cancer," he had said. "The biopsy confirmed what the doctor predicted."

Everything in me turned to mush. But since then, Lord, you have quieted our fears. Today we know the cancer is small and slow growing and does not require surgery or chemotherapy. We can resume our lives and include the treatment of our choice in our daily routine.

YOU HAVE given me a new understanding of the meaning of the phrase "the big *C.*" Now I know that it also stands for Care and Compassion—the kind only you can dispense.

Run, Grandma, Run

Dear God:

July 10, 2001. What a day! I'll not forget it. I'm exhausted, but I want to go over what happened and thank you for being with me all the way. Fifteen minutes before Josh's flight departed, he was called to the ticket counter. The attendant said the connecting flight in Atlanta had been cancelled and there was no way for my grandson to get out of that city that night. Then in the next breath he told Josh he had just booked him with another airline ...

... that his luggage would be sent to him ...

... that he was going to Charlotte, North Carolina, instead of Atlanta, Georgia ...

... that he'd be there in two and a half hours instead of thirty-five minutes!

He stopped the avalanche of information long enough to print two copies of the new itinerary. Then he punched some keys on the computer keypad.

"Oh, no," he said in surprise, "this is an awarded ticket! That means we have to give the other airline printed tickets," he continued, "so stop at our airline counter first, see the man I just called, ask him to issue the ticket, then *run* to the other airline counter, ask for the gate number and *keep running* to concourse A. It's all the way on the other side of the airport. The flight leaves in five minutes. *Go!*"

I grabbed the papers and told my grandson to run but "be careful," and I took off to make the exchange. Good thing he's thirteen and has long legs! I could have used a pair myself.

At the first counter I approached the security guard directly. "This is an emergency," I said. "I have to be in concourse A in five minutes. Please—let me go to the head of the line."

He nodded in agreement and ushered me to the front. I placed two papers on the counter.

"Flight was cancelled," I uttered, breathing hard, "need ticket for other airline."

The agent hastily wrote out the ticket, then instructed me as if I were the student and he was a teacher. "If there's a line at the next counter don't stop, just yell, 'What gate is flight 188 leaving from?' and keep on running."

I'm no athlete and it's been a "few" years since I was a teenager, but I made time that day. I just kept running. The boys at Nike would have been proud of me! I cleared the security checkpoints and tackled the last stretch. The counter was empty. The plane was about to take off. I plopped the papers on the counter and pointed out the window behind the desk. "My grandson is *going* on that *plane!*" I shouted.

The rep took one look at me and knew I was serious. By then I was gasping for air. He stamped the ticket and pushed Josh toward the jetway, no questions asked.

"Love you," I called to Josh. "Come again real soon."

"Love you, too," he said, and then he was gone.

I began walking back through the terminal. I couldn't believe how far and how fast I had run and how many things could've gone wrong on the way.

But you were there, running ahead of me, Lord, clearing the aisles, putting the right people in the right places at the right time. Thank you!

I KNOW YOU'RE the one who transported me and the one who took care of Josh all the way home. What a moment—for this senior!

Growing Old Gracefully

Dear God:

Here I am. As I write this, my feelings are fluctuating. Who would have thought a few years ago that Dan and I would be off the farm and living in a retirement community? Never dreamed of it, even.

I miss our home of nearly fifty years. But we're here—not only in our new place but in a new place in life, older and less independent than we once were. I know this suits our abilities, and I want to be content with the way it is, not looking back at the way it was.

I'm so grateful, God, for your tender mercies—new every morning. Already so many good things have occurred. We've met friendly neighbors. There are almost unlimited opportunities for helping others through volunteer work. It's also safe here, and there is plenty of time for fun and socializing. I can plant a small garden. There's help just around the corner in case of an emergency, and the surroundings are quiet and beautiful. It feels good sometimes to sit, to be still, to know that you are in charge of our lives.

Yes, I can live a full life here with other Christians who share my love for you.

LORD, YOU HAVE supplied all our needs in abundance even into old age (Phil 4:19).

To the Reader:

Do you have a senior moment you could share with me for possible publication?

If so, please e-mail me at karen@karenoconnor.com

I hope to hear from you!

Karen O' Connor